CROCHET JOURNEY

A GLOBAL CROCHET ADVENTURE FROM THE GUY WITH THE HOOK

MARK ROSEBOOM

DAVID & CHARLES

www.davidandcharles.com

MAP OF CONTENTS

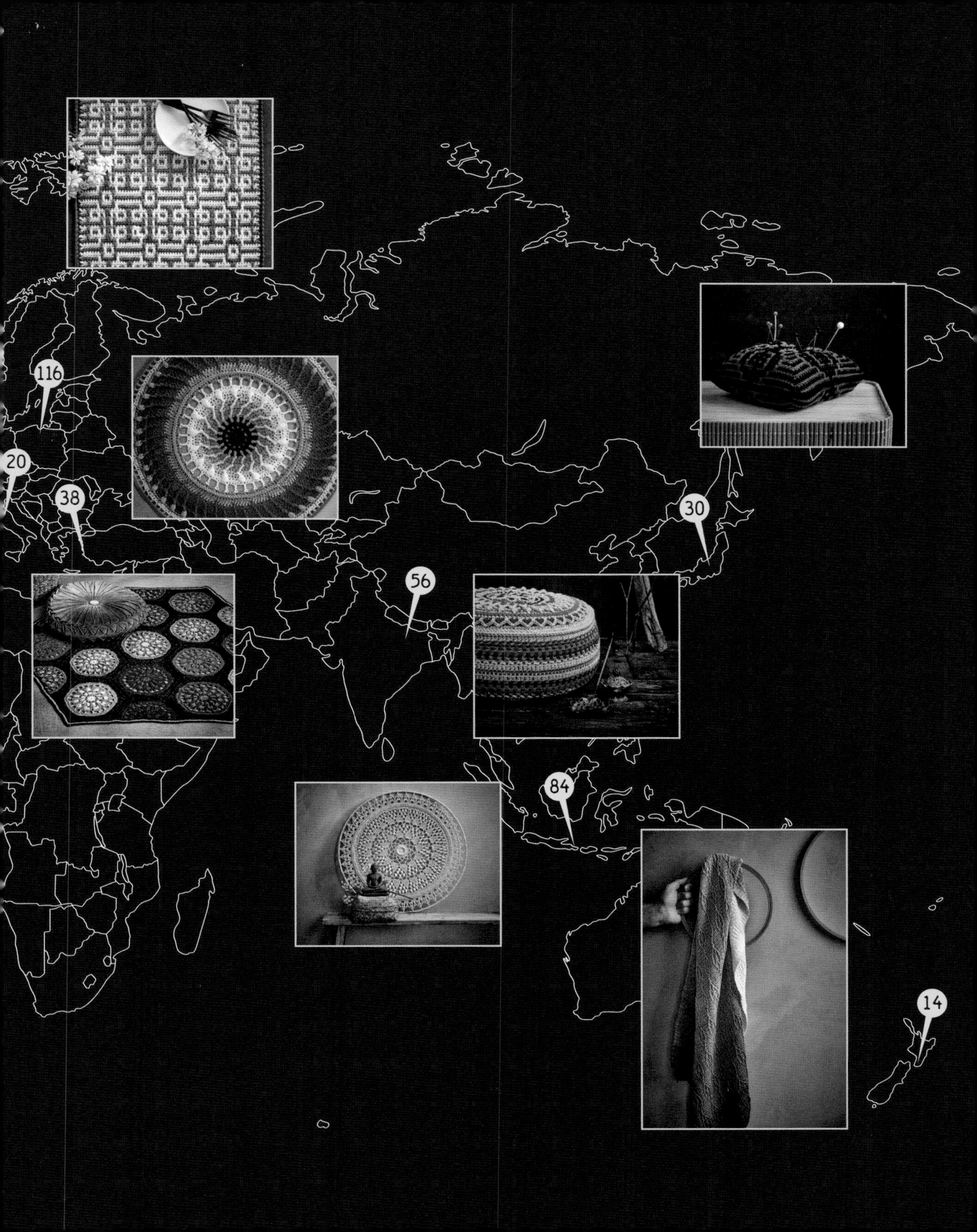
116
20
38
56
30
84
14

SOME PERSONAL WORDS BEFORE YOU START YOUR JOURNEY...

I understand that you're keen to start exploring the pages of this book, dive into the patterns I've created, and read the stories of my travels. However, there are some things I'd like to say before you do that.
I have two main passions in life that have helped me develop as a person–traveling and crochet. Both of these have helped me to grow on many levels and have given me experiences that have made me stronger and wiser over the years.

For the past decade, I've spent my days working for just one reason–to save money to buy a ticket to an unknown destination. The world has always fascinated me; there is always so much to explore and learn from in each place you visit. This might simply be your village or country, or it could be a destination thousands of miles away. My goal was to visit the rarest and most unique places in our world and soak up all the culture, lessons, and experiences that each place delivered. We can learn so much from finding out about other religions, cultures, and ways of life, and doing this has given me some of the most memorable experiences of my life; I saw little miracles happen and cherished even the smallest of things. For me, traveling doesn't mean being in the best places, staying at a five-star hotel, or wandering around the tourist trails. Often people find this is their comfort zone, but I always relish the adventure of taking another road or path which isn't that obvious. I like to see how locals do things and see unexplored nature and small wonders around me. My travel experiences have turned me into the person I am today.

As well as traveling as much as I can, I also crochet and knit and have done for a long time now. Working with yarn has always been my meditation moment of the day. We often experience daily life as being busy, full of people who want something from us, and full of tasks we set ourselves to finish. When I take my crochet hook and start designing, it's like I enter another dimension where nobody can reach out to or join me. It is my little zen-bubble. For this reason, it has always been important to me to keep a balance in my daily life; however, a few years ago I started designing, and this took me in a different direction. My meditation moment became work and, as a result, the balance was off. It took some time to get this balance back and restore the peace I had in my mind when I crochet. Nowadays, crocheting gives me the same comfort that it used to, even when I design and work out my patterns. That same inner sense of calm gave me the idea to merge my two passions, and this book is the result.

Between these pages you can enjoy my designs and my most treasured travel stories. Each pattern is inspired by a memory I have, so this book is something very personal and precious to me. I hope you enjoy crocheting the patterns and reading my travel tales from all over the world.

Mark

GENERAL TIPS AND TRICKS FOR THE PATTERNS IN THIS BOOK

Left-handed crocheters
As I am a left-handed crocheter, I know how difficult it can sometimes be to crochet from a pattern. When writing and drawing out my designs, I always like to make sure my work is mirrored in order to make it easier to follow for both left- and right-handers. So, if you are left-handed, make sure you read the diagrams and charts in this book the opposite way. If you find this hard, a small mirror will help you see the correct version for a left-handed crocheter. When crocheting patterns in the Round, your result will have to be mirrored.

The use of a magic loop
To start many of the patterns in this book, you will need to make a magic loop. Although this this a very well-known technique, if you have trouble making one as a beginner, then you don't need to use one. You can simply use the old-fashioned method of making ch6 and working a ss into the first ch of the 6. In this way, you create a ring to start your work. Decide for yourself if you need a smaller or larger circle to begin with if you decide not to use a magic loop.

Turning the work between Rows
Some of the patterns in this book are made with Rows, where you switch between working the Right Side and the Wrong Side of the work. These patterns will direct you to turn at the end of each Row.
When you turn, if the next Row starts with a single crochet then make one chain. If the Row starts with a stitch made up of chains, then there is no need to work an extra chain as you turn.

Putting colors or yarn aside
Some patterns in the book are made with different colors of yarn. In order to avoid having lots of ends to weave in, I created a technique whereby you put the color you're working with aside for a moment and pick it up later in a new Row/Round. Use this technique after the last stitch of a Row/Round when the pattern tells you to put the color aside. Once the final stitch is made, pull up the last loop into a giant circle so that the whole yarn ball can be pulled through the circle. Now pull the thread to close the loop slowly. Your ball of yarn is still attached to your work – but without the danger that it will pull out your entire Row/Round. Once the pattern tells you to pick this color back up, grab the thread and pull it through the indicated stitch. If you would like a more visual approach to this technique, you can see a tutorial on my website: www.theguywiththehook.com.

Starting the first stitch on a Row/Round
Every stitch you start within any pattern of the book will contain a ch. When making an sc, you will make a ch to gain height – but it will never count as a stitch. For other stitches, you will crochet the number of stitches needed to make it a first stitch. However, if you know how to make standing stitches, it is perfectly fine to use them at the start.

Stitch knowledge
I have decided not to fill a large part of the book with tutorials on how to make various stitches. You can find plenty of tutorials for each stitch and technique in other crochet books or online so I felt it wasn't necessary to include tutorials in this book.

Total yardage for a pattern
Each pattern in the book has information on what colors, yarn, and amounts are used. These amounts are based on the yarn suggested and the crochet hook size advised. If you decide to be creative and do it differently, this information will no longer be accurate.

Sizes
Each pattern has a finished measurement for the project, which is often achieved by blocking the item. The size is just an indication as everyone's tension in crochet can be different. It also depends on the crochet hook size you decide to use and the yarn you choose.

Blocking
For most of the patterns, I advise blocking them when finished. The best way to do this is to wash the project or let it soak in water. Block it out and pin to size while still damp using rustproof pins and leave to dry.

MAAS
WOL
MAAS
WOL
WOL
WOL

STITCH ABBREVIATIONS US

ML - Magic Loop

PUFF - make a puff stitch in or around the indicated stitch. The puff will always be closed off with a ch

PC - popcorn stitch made out of 5dc stitches and closed off with a chain

FPDTR - crochet a double treble crochet stitch around the front post of the indicated stitch

FPTR2TOG - crochet two treble crochets around the front posts of the indicated stitches together

FPTR - crochet a treble crochet stitch around the front post of the indicated stitch.

TR - treble crochet

DC3TOG - crochet 3 double crochet stitches together over the indicated stitches

DC2TOG - crochet 2 double crochet stitches together over the indicated stitches

BPDC - double crochet around the back post of the indicated stitch

FPDC2TOG - crochet two double crochet stitches around the front posts of the indicated stitches together

FPDC - double crochet stitch around the front post of the indicated stitch

2 double crochet in the same stitch

DC - double crochet

2 half double crochet in the same stitch

BPHDC - half double crochet stitch around the back post of indicated stitch.

HDC - half double crochet

SC2TOG - crochet 2 single crochet stitches together over the indicated stitches.

3 single crochet in the same stitch

2 single crochet in the same stitch

SC - single crochet

BLO - back loop only

FLO - front loop only

CH - chain

SS - slip stitch

CROSSED FPTR - crochet an fptr around the second stitch along, then make an fptr around the first stitch. For left-handed crocheters, it is the opposite – so work an fptr around the second stitch along to the right, then make an fptr around the first stitch to the right.

ST(S) - stitch(es)
SK - skip (as in skip stitch)
SP - space (as in ch2-space)
CRN - corner

* marks the start point of a repeat

[ ] gives a total amount of stitches at the end of a Round/Row

( ) phrases between round brackets indicate a stitch repeat within a Round/Row or sometimes a note

REP – repeat

GR - group

41°16'S, 174°46'E
• HILLS • FORESTS • RIVER POOLS
• CLIFFS • HIKING • CAMPING • SWIMMING

NEW ZEALAND (WELLINGTON - KAITOKE REGIONAL PARK)

RIVENDELL SHAWL

For this pattern, the inspiration came from Middle Earth, a fictional place that J.R.R. Tolkien created for his *Lord of the Rings* books. This fantasy world came to life when Peter Jackson adapted this fantastic tale for the screen. I have always loved this story and I am happy that the movies did justice to the books with regards to the locations. The rich fantasies in the story came alive and, as a result, I found the inspiration for this pattern.

Since many of the scenes were filmed in New Zealand, I knew it was the destination to go to if I wanted my dream to come true. So I arrived in Wellington, New Zealand, and took a car up to the Kaitoke Regional Park. For those of you who have seen *The Lord of the Rings*, you might recognize the Elvish city of Rivendell. The forests, nature, and décor are mostly filmed in Kaitoke Park, and once you start walking the trail, you will see the massive gate of Rivendell, which still stands there today.

On this gate, there is an engraved pattern of crossed branches with leaves. You will find a representation of these engravings in this pattern. I created the leaves of Rivendell for this shawl as a memory of this beautiful place where the trees grow tall and water rushes through the mountains.

PATTERN

R1 (WS): Ch3 (ch + first hdc), make 2hdc more in the first ch from ch3. Turn. [3hdc]

R2 (RS): Ch1 (doesn't count as st here and throughout entire pattern), 1sc in each st of Row. Turn. [3sc]

R3 (WS): Ch2 (first hdc), 1hdc in same st, 1hdc in every st of Row until the end. Turn. [4hdc]

Rep Row 2 & 3 until you reach an amount of 15hdc. It will give 22 more Rows of pattern, and in Row 25 you will make the fifteenth hdc. So, we continue with Row 26.

R26 (RS): Ch1, 1sc in next 5 sts, 1fptr around sc two Rows down, sk st on current Row, 1sc in next 9 sts. Turn. [14sc/1fptr]

R27 and all further odd Rows (WS): Rep Row 3. [16hdc]

R28 (RS): Ch1, 1sc in next 4 sts, 1fptr around fptr two Rows down, sk st on current Row, 1sc in next 2 sts, 1fptr around the same fptr you just used, sk st on current Row, 1sc in next 8 sts. Turn. [14sc/2fptr]

R30 (RS): Ch1, 1sc in next 3 sts, (1fptr around fptr two Rows down, sk st on current Row, 1sc in next st, 1fptr around the same fptr you just used, sk st on current Row) twice. 1sc in next 8 sts. Turn. [13sc/4fptr]

R32 (RS): Ch1, 1sc in next 3 sts, 1fptr around fptr two Rows down, sk st on current Row, 1sc in next st, 1 crossed fptr over next two fptr stitches two Rows down, sk 2 sts on current Row, 1sc in next st, 1fptr around next fptr two Rows down, sk st on current Row, 1sc in next 9 sts. Turn. [14sc/4fptr]

R34 (RS): Ch1, 1sc in next 3 sts, 1fptr around fptr two Rows down, sk st on current Row, 1sc in next st, 1 crossed fptr over next two fptr stitches two Rows down, sk **2 sts on** current Row, 1sc in next st, 1fptr around next fptr two Rows down, sk st on current Row, 1sc in next 10 sts. Turn. [15sc/4fptr]

R36 (RS): Ch1, 1sc in next 4 sts, 1fptr2tog over next 2 fptr stitches two Rows down, sk st on current Row, 1sc in next 2 sts, 1fptr2tog over next 2 fptr stitches two Rows down, sk st on current Row, 1sc in next 12 sts. Turn. [18sc/2 x fptr2tog]

R38 (RS): Ch1, 1sc in next 5 sts, (1fptr around fptr2tog two Rows down, sk st on current Row) twice, 1sc in next 14 sts. Turn. [19sc/2fptr]

R40 (RS): Ch1, 1sc in next 5 sts, 1 crossed fptr over next two fptr two Rows down, sk 2 sts on current Row, 1sc in next 15 sts. Turn. [20sc/2fptr]

HOOK SIZE NEEDED: 4.0MM (G/6) HOOK

YARN NEEDED: SCHEEPJES WHIRL 755 BLUEBERRY BAMBAM. SCHEEPJES WHIRL COMES IN CAKES OF 215G (7½OZ) WITH A LENGTH OF 1000M (1093½YDS) OF YARN. THE YARN CONSISTS OF 60% COTTON AND 40% ACRYLIC.

SIZE OF PROJECT: WINGSPAN 165CM (65IN), SHORTEST SIDE 76CM (30IN), WIDEST SIDE 145CM (57IN).

R42 (RS): Ch1, 1sc in next 5 sts, 1 crossed fptr over two fptr stitches of the crossed fptr stitches two Rows down, sk 2 sts on current Row, 1sc in next 6 sts, 1fptr around sc two Rows down, sk st on current Row, 1sc in next 9 sts. Turn. [20sc/3fptr]

R44 (RS): Ch1, 1sc in next 4 sts, 1fptr around the first fptr of crossed fptr two Rows down, sk st on current Row, 1sc in next 2 sts, 1fptr around the second fptr of crossed fptr, sk st on current Row, 1sc in next 4 sts, 1fptr around next fptr two Rows down, sk st on current Row, 1sc in next 2 sts, 1fptr around the same fptr you just used, sk st on current Row, 1sc in next 8 sts. Turn. [20sc/4fptr]

R46 (RS): Ch1, 1sc in next 2 sts, * 1sc in next st, (1fptr around next fptr two Rows down, sk st on current Row, 1sc in next st, 1fptr around the same fptr you just used, sk st on current Row) 2 times, 1 sc in next st. **Rep from* 1 more time.** 1sc in next 7 sts. Turn. [17sc/8fptr]

TIPS FOR THIS PATTERN:

- ALL ODD ROWS WILL BE CROCHETED THE SAME AS ROW 3 (WITH HDC STITCHES)
- IN EVERY ODD ROW, YOU WILL INCREASE ONE ST ON THE WINGSPAN BY WORKING THE BEGINNING CH2 AND AN HDC IN THE SAME ST. ON EACH EVEN ROW THERE ARE NO INCREASES.
- SPECIAL STITCH: 4FPTR-CLUSTER - CROCHET 4 FRONT POST TREBLE STS AROUND THE INDICATED ST, THEN FINISH AS A REGULAR POPCORN ST. ALWAYS CROCHET A CH AFTER THE CLUSTER IS CLOSED.

R48 (RS): Ch1, 1sc in next 2 sts, * 1sc in next st, 1fptr around next fptr two Rows down, sk st on current Row, 1sc in next st, 1 crossed fptr around next 2 fptr stitches two Rows down, sk 2 sts on current Row, 1sc in next st, 1fptr around next fptr two Rows down, sk st on current Row, 1sc in next st. **Rep from * 1 more time.** 1sc in next 8 sts. Turn. [18sc/8fptr]

R50 (RS): Ch1, 1sc in next 2 sts, * 1sc in next st, 1fptr around next fptr two Rows down, sk st on current Row, 1sc in next st, 1 crossed fptr around next 2 fptr stitches two Rows down, sk 2 sts on current Row, 1sc in next st, 1fptr around next fptr two Rows down, sk st on current Row, 1sc in next st. **Rep from * 1 more time.** 1sc in next 9 sts. Turn. [19sc/8fptr]

R52 (RS): Ch1, 1sc in next 2 sts, * 1sc in next 2 sts, (1 fptr2tog over next 2 fptr stitches two Rows down, sk st on current Row, 1sc in next 2 sts) twice. **Rep from * 1 more time.** 1sc in next 10 sts. Turn. [24sc/4 x fptr2tog]

R54 (RS): Ch1, 1sc in next 2 sts, * 1sc in next 3 sts, (1fptr around first fptr2tog two Rows down, sk st on current Row) twice, 1sc in next 3 sts. **Rep from * 1 more time.** 1sc in next 11 sts. Turn. [25sc/4fptr]

R56 (RS): Ch1, 1sc in next 2 sts, * 1sc in next 3 sts, 1 crossed fptr over next 2 fptr stitches two Rows down, sk 2 sts on current Row, 1sc in next 3 sts. **Rep from * 1 more time.** 1sc in next 12 sts. Turn. [26sc/4fptr]

R58 (RS): Ch1, 1sc in next 2 sts, * 1sc in next 3 sts, 1 crossed fptr over 2 fptr stitches of the crossed fptr two Rows down, sk 2 sts on current Row, 1sc in next 3 sts. **Rep from * 1 more time.** 1sc in next 3 sts, 1 fptr around sc two Rows down, sk st on current Row, 1sc in next 9 sts. Turn. [26sc/5fptr]

R60 (RS): Ch1, 1sc in next 2 sts, * 1sc in next 2 sts, (1fptr around next fptr two Rows down, sk st on current Row, 1sc in next 2 sts) 2 times. **Rep from * 1 more time.** 1sc in next 2 sts, 1fptr around next fptr two Rows down, sk st on current Row, 1sc in next 2 sts, 1fptr around the same fptr you just used, sk st on current Row, 1sc in next 8 sts. Turn. [26sc/6fptr]

From this point, it is only a matter of repeating the Rows we just made. The only thing changing is the number of reps completed in a Row. The bold part in the Rows will change in numbers, and only the totals and Rows will be named in the next parts.

In the next Rows, the rep part goes from 1 rep to 2.
R62: Rep R46 [21sc/12fptr]
R64: Rep R48 [22sc/12fptr]
R66: Rep R50 [23sc/12fptr]
R68: Rep R52 [30sc/6 x fptr2tog]
R70: Rep R54 [31sc/6fptr]
R72: Rep R56 [32sc/6fptr]
R74: Rep R58 [32sc/7fptr]
R76: Rep R60 [32sc/8fptr]

In the next Rows, the rep part goes from 1 rep to 3.
R78: Rep R46 [25sc/16fptr]
R80: Rep R48 [26sc/16fptr]
R82: Rep R50 [27sc/16fptr]
R84: Rep R52 [36sc/8 x fptr2tog]
R86: Rep R54 [37sc/8fptr]
R88: Rep R56 [38sc/8fptr]
R90: Rep R58 [38sc/9fptr
R92: Rep R60 [38sc/10fptr]

In the next Rows, the rep part goes from 1 rep to 4.
R94: Rep R46 [29sc/20fptr]
R96: Rep R48 [30sc/20fptr]
R98: Rep R50 [31sc/20fptr]
R100: Rep R52 [42sc/10 x fptr2tog]
R102: Rep R54 [43sc/10fptr]
R104: Rep R56 [44sc/10fptr]
R106: Rep R58 [44sc/11fptr]
R108: Rep R60 [44sc/12fptr]

In the next Rows, the rep part goes from 1 rep to 5.
R110: Rep R46 [33sc/24fptr]
R112: Rep R48 [34sc/24fptr]
R114: Rep R50 [35sc/24fptr]
R116: Rep R52 [48sc/12 x fptr2tog]
R118: Rep R54 [49sc/12fptr]
R120: Rep R56 [50sc/12fptr]
R122: Rep R58 [50sc/13ptr]
R124: Rep R60 [50sc/14fptr]

In the next Rows, the rep part goes from 1 rep to 6.
R126: Rep R46 [37sc/28fptr]
R128: Rep R48 [38sc/28fptr]
R130: Rep R50 [39sc/28fptr]
R132: Rep R52 [54sc/14 x fptr2tog]
R134: Rep R54 [55sc/14fptr]
R136: Rep R56 [56sc/14fptr]
R138: Rep R58 [56sc/15fptr]
R140: Rep R60 [56sc/16fptr]

In the next Rows, the rep part goes from 1 rep to 7.
R142: Rep R46 [41sc/32fptr]
R144: Rep R48 [42sc/32fptr]
R146: Rep R50 [43sc/32fptr]
R148: Rep R52 [60sc/16 x fptr2tog]
R150: Rep R54 [61sc/16fptr]
R152: Rep R56 [62sc/16fptr]
R154: Rep R58 [62sc/17fptr]
R156: Rep R60 [62sc/18fptr]

In the next Rows, the rep part goes from 1 rep to 8.
R158: Rep R46 [45sc/36fptr]
R160: Rep R48 [46sc/36fptr]
R162: Rep R50 [47sc/36fptr]
R164: Rep R52 [66sc/18 x fptr2tog]
R166: Rep R54 [67sc/18fptr]
R168: Rep R56 [68sc/18fptr]
R170: Rep R58 [68sc/19fptr]
R172: Rep R60 [68sc/20fptr]

In the next Rows, the rep part goes from 1 rep to 9.
R174: Rep R46 [49sc/40fptr]
R176: Rep R48 [50sc/40fptr]
R178: Rep R50 [51sc/40fptr]
R180: Rep R52 [72sc/20 x fptr2tog]
R182: Rep R54 [73sc/20fptr]
R184: Rep R56 [74sc/20fptr]
R186: Rep R58 [74sc/21fptr]
R188: Rep R60 [74sc/22fptr]

R188: Rep R60 [74sc/22fptr]

In the next Rows, the rep part goes from 1 rep to 10.
R190: Rep R46 [53sc/44fptr]
R192: Rep R48 [54sc/44fptr]
R194: Rep R50 [55sc/44fptr]
R196: Rep R52 [78sc/22 x fptr2tog]
R198: Rep R54 [79sc/22fptr]
R200: Rep R56 [80sc/22fptr]
R202: Rep R58 [80sc/23fptr]
R204: Rep R60 [80sc/24fptr]

THIS SHAWL IS A MEMORY OF THAT BEAUTIFUL PLACE WHERE THE TREES GROW TALL AND WATER IS RUSHING THROUGH THE MOUNTAINS

In the next Rows, the rep part goes from 1 rep to 11.
R206: Rep R46 [57sc/48fptr]
R208: Rep R48 [58sc/48fptr]
R210: Rep R50 [59sc/48fptr]
R212: Rep R52 [84sc/24 x fptr2tog]
R214: Rep R54 [85sc/24fptr]
R216: Rep R56 [86sc/24fptr]
R218: Rep R58 [86sc/25fptr]
R220: Rep R60 [86sc/26fptr]

In the next Rows, the rep part goes from 1 rep to 12.
R222: Rep R46 [61sc/52fptr]
R224: Rep R48 [62sc/52fptr]
R226: Rep R50 [63sc/52fptr]
R228: Rep R52 [90sc/26 x fptr2tog]
R230: Rep R54 [91sc/26fptr]
R232: Rep R56 [92sc/26fptr]
R234: Rep R58 [92sc/27fptr]
R236: Rep R60 [92sc/28fptr]

In the next Rows, the rep part goes from 1 rep to 13.
R238: Rep R46 [65sc/56fptr]
R240: Rep R48 [66sc/56fptr]
R242: Rep R50 [67sc/56fptr]
R244: Rep R52 [96sc/28 x fptr2tog]
R246: Rep R54 [97sc/28fptr]

R248 (RS): Ch1, 1sc in next 2 sts, * 1sc in next 3 sts, 1fptr around both fptr stitches two Rows down, sk st on current Row, 1sc in next 4 sts. **Rep from * 13 times more.** 1sc in next 12 sts. Turn. [112sc/14fptr]

R250 (RS): Ch1, 1sc in next 2 sts, * 1sc in next 11 sts, 1fptr around next fptr two Rows down, sk st on current Row, 1sc in next 4 sts. **Rep from * 6 more times.** 1sc in next 13 sts. Turn. [120sc/7fptr]

R252 (RS): Ch1, 1sc in next 2 sts, * 1sc in next 11 sts, 4fptr-cluster around fptr two Rows down, sk st on current Row, 1sc in next 4 sts. **Rep from * 6 more times.** 1sc in next 14 sts. Turn. [121sc/7 x 4fptr-cluster]

R254 (RS): Ch1, 1sc in each st on Row until the end. Turn. [129sc]

Rep R253 and 254 until all the yarn is used.
Fasten off yarn. Weave in the ends.

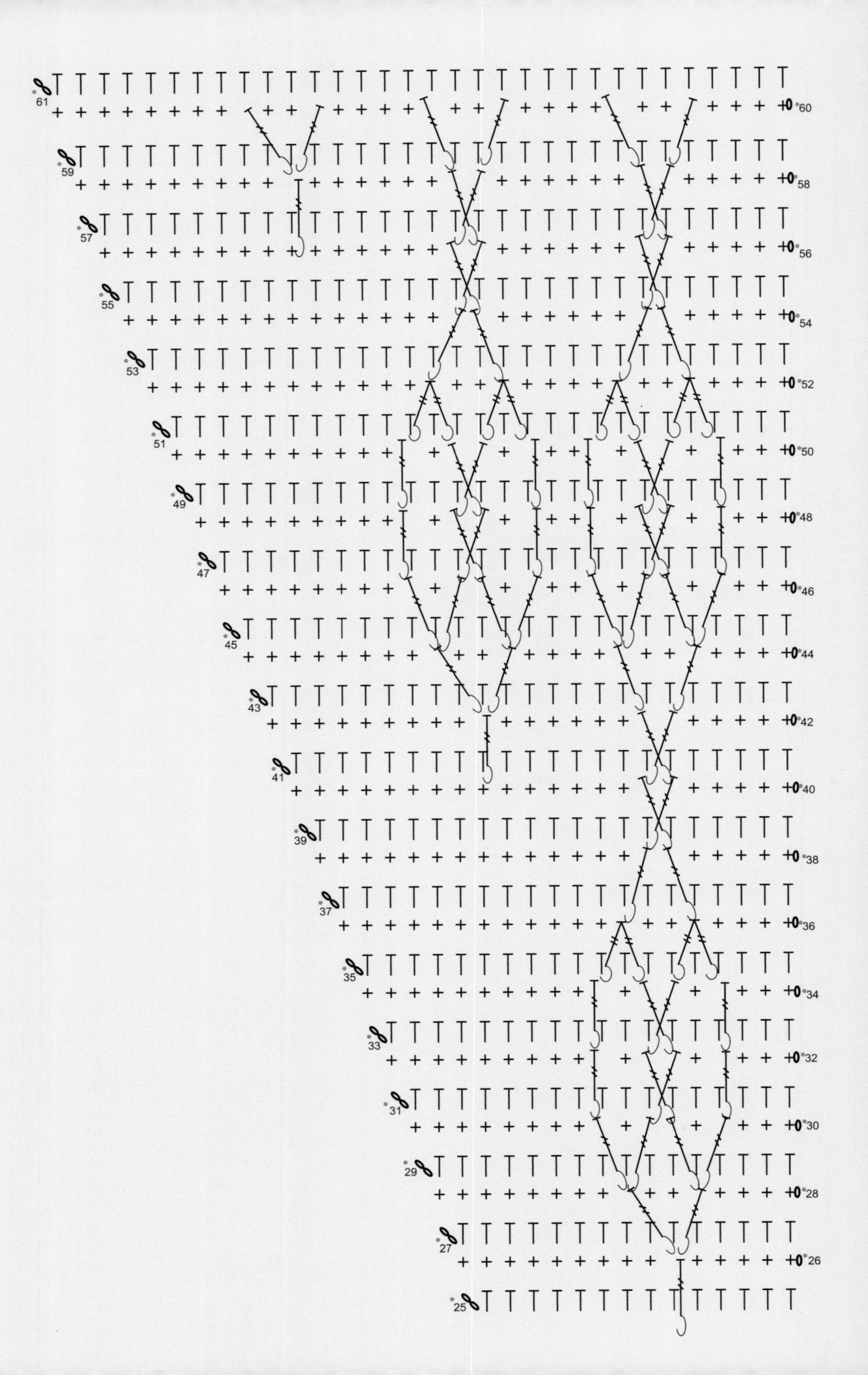
61
60
59
58
57
56
55
54
53
52
51
50
49
48
47
46
45
44
43
42
41
40
39
38
37
36
35
34
33
32
31
30
29
28
27
26
25

THIS PATTERN
FEATURES THE
ENGRAVINGS
ON THE STONE
WALLS OF
RIVENDELL

41°54'N, 12°29'E
• BASILICA • LANDMARK • MOSAIC
• ESQUILINE HILL • FRESCOES

ITALY (ROME – SANTA MARIA MAGGIORE CATHEDRAL)

SANTA MARIA MAGGIORE RUG

"All roads lead to Rome," they say. And honestly, I think everyone should visit Rome at least once in their life. The city is full of history and architectural highlights and is an experience not to be missed – it also has excellent coffee and pasta of course! A city trip becomes more memorable if you turn off the tourist trail and discover the hidden gems. Sometimes you'll find them by accident, as I did when I visited Rome and found the inspiration for this pattern.

I was walking back to the guesthouse from a visit to the Vatican. The sky was dark gray and suddenly it started raining. And when it rains in Rome, it really rains! So I searched for a place to shelter. I walked past a cathedral called the Santa Maria Maggiore, which was open, and I walked in. From the moment I stepped into this church, something magical happened.

The thunder started, and its sound was rolling deep through the church. As there was a service going on, I could hear the gentle sound of hymns being sung. I sat down on a wooden bench in the middle of the church – it was a magical feeling to hear the soft melodies in the background, hear the rain pouring down outside, and see the white, flashing lights of the thunder. Each time a flash of thunder appeared, the mosaic window full of color in the back of the church was reflected onto the marble floor in silhouette, showing all the beautiful details. It happened repeatedly, and it left a strong image in my mind, which stayed with me long after the rain was gone. I have tried to capture the stained-glass silhouette in this rug, from the image in my mind.

THE WHOLE HEXAGON MOTIF

With Color A and crochet hook size 4.0mm (G/6), make a ML.

R1 (RS): Ch3 (first dc), make 11dc more in the loop. Ss in top of first st to connect. Put Color A aside. [12dc]

R2: Take Color B and attach it in any st. ch5 (first dc + ch2), (1dc in next st, ch2) 11 times. Ss in the third ch to connect. Put Color B aside. [12dc/12 x ch2-sp]

R3: Pick up Color A in any ch2-sp. Ch3 (first dc of the first pc), make 4dc more in ch2-sp and join them with the ch3 to make a pc st, ch3, sk next st, (1pc in next ch2-sp, ch3, sk next st) 11 times. Ss in top of the first pc to connect. Put Color A aside. [12pc/12 x ch3-sp]

R4: Pick up Color B in any ch3-sp. Ch1 (doesn't count as st here and throughout entire pattern), *1sc in ch3-sp, 1fpdtr around dc from Round 2, 1sc in the same ch3-sp, ch4, sk next pc. Rep from * 11 more times. Ss in top of first st to connect. Put Color B aside. [24sc/12 fpdtr/ 12 x ch4-sp]

R5: Pick up Color A in any ch4-sp. Ch1, *1sc-2dc-1tr-ch1-1tr-2dc-1sc in ch4-sp, sk all sts to the next ch4-sp. Rep from * 11 more times. Ss in top of first st to connect. Put Color A aside. [12 gr of sc/2dc/tr/ch1/tr/2dc/sc]

R6: Pick up Color B in any ch1-sp between two tr. Ch4 (first hdc + ch2), make 1hdc in same sp, 1sc in next 2 sts, 1fpdtr around fpdtr from Round 4, ch3, 1fpdtr around same fpdtr you just used, sk next 4 sts on current Round (dc/2sc/dc), 1sc in next 2 sts. *1hdc-ch2-1hdc in next ch1-sp, 1sc in next 2 sts, 1fpdtr around fpdtr from Round 4, ch3, 1fpdtr around same fpdtr you just used, sk next 4 sts on current Round (dc/2sc/dc), 1sc in next 2 sts. Rep from * 10 more times. Ss in top of second ch to connect. Put Color B aside. [12 gr of 2sc/hdc/ch/hdc/2sc and 12 gr of fpdtr/ch3/fpdtr]

R7: Pick up Color A in any ch2-sp between two hdc. Ch1, *1sc in ch2-sp, ch5, sk all sts to next ch3-sp, 1dc in ch3-sp, ch5, sk all sts to next ch2-sp. Rep from * 11 more times. Ss in top of first st to connect. Put Color A aside. [12sc/12dc/24 x ch5-sp]

R8: Pick up Color B in the closest ch5-sp. Ch2 (first hdc), make 4hdc more in the same ch5-sp, sk next st, (5hdc in next ch5-sp, sk next st) 23 times. Ss in top of first st to connect. Fasten off Color B. [120hdc]

R9: Pick up Color A in any st. Ch1, 1sc in each st on Round. Ss in top of first st to connect. Fasten off Color A. [120sc]

HOOK SIZE NEEDED: 4.0MM (G/6) HOOK

YARN NEEDED: SCHEEPJES STONE WASHED/ RIVER WASHED COLOR PACK COMES WITH 10G (⅓OZ) BALLS, WITH A LENGTH OF 26M (28YDS) OF YARN PER BALL.

- 38 BALLS ASSORTED COLORS
- SCHEEPJES STONE WASHED COMES IN BALLS OF 50G (1¾OZ) WITH A LENGTH OF 130M (142YDS) OF YARN. IT CONSISTS OF 78% COTTON/22% ACYRLIC.
- 8 BALLS OF SCHEEPJES STONE WASHED 803 BLACK ONYX
- 1 BALL OF SCHEEPJES STONE WASHED 801 MOON STONE

SIZE OF PROJECT: THE SIZE OF A WHOLE AND HALF MOTIF WILL BE 30.5CM (12IN) FROM POINT TO POINT. THE FINISHED RUG WILL BE APPROXIMATELY 120CM (47IN) FROM POINT TO POINT.

R10: Take Color C and attach it in any st. ch1, *1sc in next 3 sts, 1hdc in next 4 sts, 1dc in next 3 sts, 1dc-ch2-1dc in next st, 1dc in next 3 sts, 1hdc in next 4 sts, 1sc in next 2 sts. Rep from * 5 more times. Ss in top of first st to connect. [6 sides of 4dc/4hdc/5sc/4hdc/4dc/ch2-crn]

R11: *Starting in third sc on a side.* Ch3 (first dc), 1dc in next 10 sts, 1dc-ch2-1dc in next ch2-sp, 1dc in next 10 sts. *1dc in next 11 sts, 1dc-ch2-1dc in next ch2-sp, 1dc in next 10 sts. Rep from * 4 more times. Ss in top of first st to connect. [6 sides of 23dc and a ch2-crn]

R12: Ch2 (no st, only used to get to the back of your work), *1bpdc around next 12 sts, 1dc-ch2-1dc in next ch2-sp, 1bpdc around next 11 sts. Rep from * 5 more times. Ss in top of first st to connect. Fasten off Color C. [6 sides of 23bpdc/2dc and a ch2-crn]

Weave in all ends and block motif before joining.

The Half Hexagon Motif will be worked in Rows instead of Rounds. The entire motif will be crocheted on the Right Side of the work except Row 11, which is worked on the WS.

TIPS FOR THIS PATTERN:

- IN THIS PATTERN, I USE FOUR COLORS. COLORS A AND B ONE OF THE 38 BALLS OF 10G (⅓OZ) OF STONE WASHED AND RIVER WASHED YARNS. JUST MAKE COMBINATIONS OF TWO OUT OF YOUR CHOICE IN 19 PAIRS. OUT OF THESE 19 PAIRS, YOU MAKE 13 WHOLE MOTIFS AND 6 HALF MOTIFS OF THE PATTERN. COLOR C IS THE BLACK PRIMARY COLOR, AND COLOR D IS THE WHITE COLOR FOR THE BORDER.
- THIS PATTERN CAN EASILY BE CHANGED IN FORM OR SIZE AS YOU WORK WITH MOTIFS.
- •• ALL ROUNDS/ROWS IN THIS PATTERN WILL BE WORKED ON THE RIGHT SIDE OF THE WORK - EXCEPT ROW 11 OF THE HALF HEXAGON MOTIF.
- AS THE MOTIFS HAVE SOME LACEWORK IN THEM, THEY CAN RUFFLE A BIT AFTER FINISHING. BLOCK THE MOTIFS BEFORE JOINING FOR THE BEST OUTCOME.

PATTERN HALF HEXAGON MOTIF

With Color A and hook size 4.0mm (G/6), make a ML.

R1 (RS): Ch3 (first dc), make 5dc more in the loop. Fasten off. [6dc]

R2: Take Color B and attach it to the first st of the last Row. Ch5 (first dc + ch2), (1dc in next st, ch2) 4 times. 1dc in last st. Fasten off yarn. [6dc/5 x ch2-sp]

R3: Take Color A and attach in first st of last Row (which will be third ch). Ch6 (first dc + ch3), (1pc in next ch2-sp, sk next st, ch3) 4 times. 1pc in next ch2-sp, ch3, 1 dc in last st. Fasten off. [5pc/2dc/6 x ch3-sp]

R4: Take Color B and attach in first st of last Row (which will be the third ch). Ch1, 1sc in st. * 1sc in next ch3-sp, 1fpdtr around dc of Row 2, 1sc in same ch3-sp, ch4, sk next pc. Rep from * 4 more times. 1sc in next ch3-sp, 1fpdtr around dc of Row 2, 1sc in the same ch3-sp, 1sc in last st on Row. Fasten off. [14sc/6fpdtr]

R5: Take Color A and attach it to the first st of the last Row. It will be the first sc made in the last Row. Ch4 (first tr), 2dc, and make a sc in the same st. (sk all sts to next ch4-sp, 1sc/2dc/tr/ch1/tr/2dc/1sc in ch4-sp) 5 times, sk all sts to last st on Row, 1sc-2dc-tr in last st. Fasten off. [5 gr of sc/2dc/tr/ch1/tr/2dc/sc and 2 half gr of tr/2dc/sc]

R6: Take Color B and attach in first st of last Row. This will be the first tr made in last Row. Ch2 (first hdc), 1sc in same st, 1sc in next st. * 1fpdtr around fpdtr of Row 4, ch3, 1fpdtr around same fpdtr you just used, sk next 4 sts on current Row (dc/2sc/dc), 1sc in next 2 sts, 1hdc-ch2-1hdc in ch1-sp, 1sc in next 2 sts. Rep from * 4 more times. 1fpdtr around fpdtr on Row 4, ch3, 1fpdtr around fpdtr you just used, sk next 4 sts on current Row, 1sc in next st, 1sc-1hdc in last st on Row. Fasten off. [24sc/12hdc/5 x ch2-sp/12fpdtr/6 x ch3-sp]

R7: Take Color A and attach it to the first st of the last Row. It will be the first sc made in the last Row. Ch1, 1sc in st, ch5, sk all sts to next ch3-sp, (1dc in ch3-sp, ch5, sk all sts to next ch2-sp, 1sc in next ch2-sp, ch5, sk all sts to next ch3-sp) 5 times. 1dc in next ch3-sp, ch5, sk all sts to last st on Row, 1sc in last st. Fasten off. [7sc/6dc/12 x ch5-sp]

R8: Take Color B and attach it to the first st of the last Row. It will be the first sc made in the last Row. Ch2 (first hdc), 5hdc in next ch5-sp, (sk next st, 5hdc in next ch5-sp) 11 times, 1hdc in last st on Row. Fasten off. [62hdc]

R9: Take Color A and attach it to the first st of the last Row. It will be the first hdc made in the previous Row. Ch1, 1sc in each st on Row. Fasten off. [62sc]

R10: Take Color C and attach it to the first st of the last Row. It will be the first sc made in the last Row. Ch3 (first dc), 1dc in next 3 sts, 1hdc in next 4 sts, 1sc in next 5 sts, 1hdc in next 4 sts, 1dc in next 3 sts, 1dc-ch2-1dc in next st, 1dc in next 3 sts, 1hdc in next 4 sts, 1sc in next 2 sts, sc2tog over next 2 sts, 1sc in next 2 sts, 1hdc in next 4 sts, 1dc in next 3 sts, 1dc-ch2-1dc in next st, 1dc in next 3 sts, 1hdc in next 4 sts, 1sc in next 5 sts, 1hdc in next 4 sts, 1dc in next 4 sts. Turn. [2 sides of 4dc/4hdc/5sc/4hdc/4dc, 1 side of 4dc/4hdc/2sc/sc2tog/2sc/4hdc/4dc and 2 x ch2-crn]

R11 (WS): Ch3 (first dc), 1dc in same st, 1dc in next 20 sts, 1dc-ch2-1dc in next ch2-sp, 1dc in next 21 sts, 1dc-ch2-1dc in next ch2-sp, 1dc in next 20 sts, 2dc in last st on Row. Turn. [3 sides of 23dc and 2 x ch2-crn]

R12 (RS): Ch3 (first dc), 1dc in same st, 1bpdc around next 22 sts, 1dc-ch2-1dc in next ch2-crn, 1bpdc around next 23 sts, 1dc-ch2-1dc in next ch2-crn, 1bpdc around next 22 sts, 2dc in last st on Row. Fasten off. [3 sides of 25 sts and 2 x ch2-crn]

Weave in all ends and block the half motif before joining for the best results.

Joining the Motifs:
To join the motifs, you need to make 13 whole hexagons and 6 half hexagons. Once you've done that, it is time to put them together. See figure 1 on how to do that. You will join all sides by making ss through stitches on both sides of the two motifs simultaneously. Corners will be combined by crocheting an sc through both

A CITY TRIP WILL BECOME MEMORABLE IF YOU TURN OFF THE TOURIST TRAIL AND DISCOVER THE HIDDEN GEMS

Figure 1

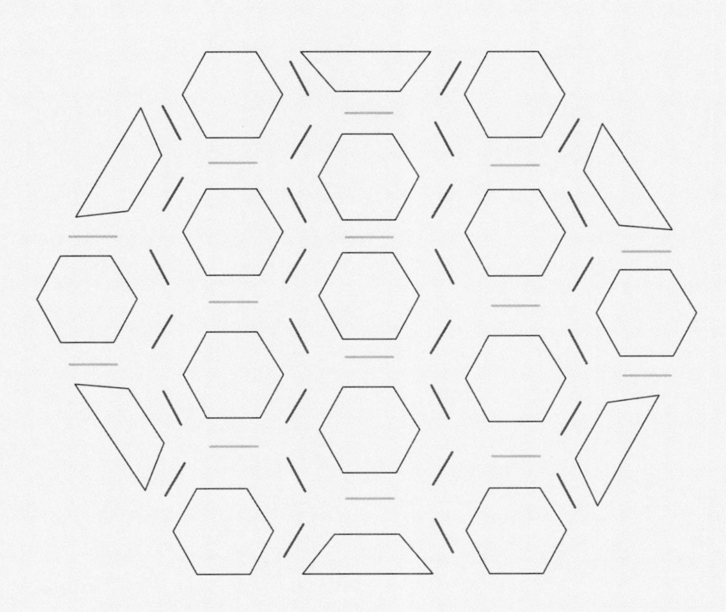

spaces of both motifs at the same time. While joining Motifs, always hold them with the RS facing each other, so you'll join them on the Wrong Side. First, join all motifs on the figure's orange lines to ends up with 5 rows of motifs. After that, connect those Rows of Motifs with the brown lines to get one big, joined Hexagon out of the motifs. Weave in all ends before starting the border.

The Border:
Take Color C and hook size 4.0mm (G/8) and attach yarn in a ch2-crn of a whole motif, which forms the start of one of the six sides of the rug.

R1 (RS): Ch5 (1dc + ch2), 1dc in same sp, 1dc in next 25 sts, 2dc in next ch2-crn, 1dc in gap between the two motifs, now make 45dc divided equally over the half motif side, 1dc in next gap between two motifs, 2dc in next ch2-crn, 1dc in next 25 sts. *1dc-ch2-1dc in next ch2-crn, 1dc in next 25 sts, 2dc in next ch2-crn, 1dc in gap between the two motifs, now make 45dc divided equally over the half motif side, 1dc in next gap between two motifs, 2dc in next ch2-crn, 1dc in next 25 sts. Rep from * 4 more times. Ss in top of the third ch to connect. Fasten off Color C. [6 sides of 103dc and 6 x ch2-crn]

R2: Take Color D and attach it in any ch2-crn. Ch4 (first hdc + ch2), 1hdc in same sp, 1hdc in next 103 sts. * 1hdc-ch2-1hdc in next ch2-crn, 1hdc in next 103 sts. Rep from * 4 more times. Ss in top of the second ch to connect. Fasten off Color D. [6 sides of 105hdc and 6 x ch2-crn]

R3: Take Color C and attach it to any ch2-crn. Ch1, * 1sc-ch2-1sc in ch2-crn, 1sc in next 105 sts. Rep from * 5 more times. Ss in top of first st to connect. Fasten off Color C. [6 sides of 107sc and 6 x ch2-crn]

Weave in all remaining ends and block the rug if necessary.

2
3
4
5
6
7
8
9
10
11
12

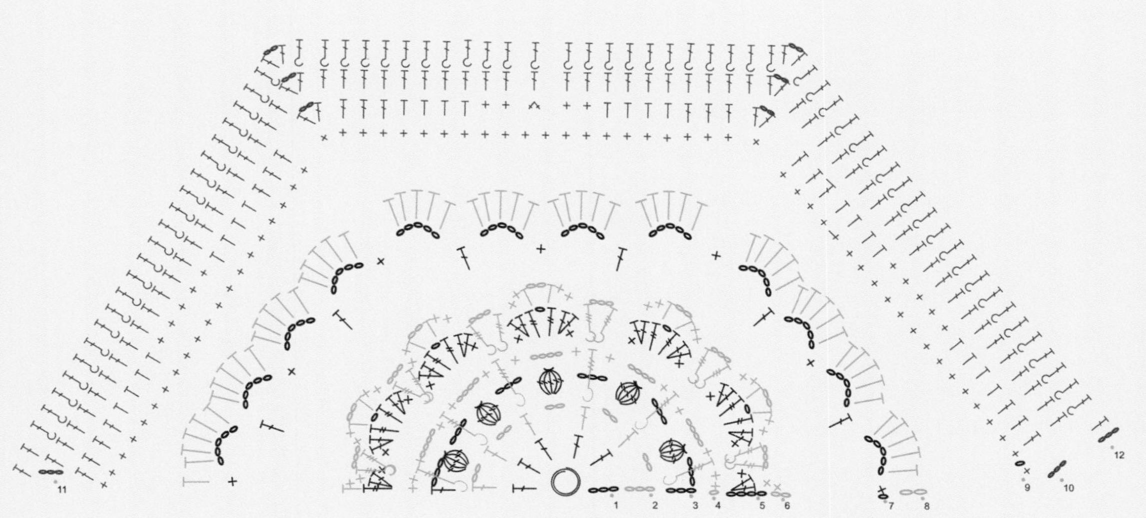
1
2
3
4
5
6
7
8
9
10
11
12

35°18'N, 139°33'E
• SAGAMI BAY • COASTAL TOWN • MOUNTAINS
• SEA • MONASTERY • FENG SHUI GARDENS

JAPAN

KAMAKURA PIN CUSHION

For this design, we go to Japan. Japan is a world of its own. There is no other country where you can find so much diversity and culture. I went in 2018 with a backpack and a train ticket. I arrived in the capital Tokyo, from there I found my way by train through the rest of the country. I visited so many exciting places, spoke to so many incredible people, and had a moment full of wonder every day. Early on in the trip I took several trains up to the south-west region just outside Tokyo, where there is a small town by the seaside named Kamakura. It is built against a mountain, and here you will find the Buddhist temple Kotuku-In, which holds one of the biggest bronze Buddha statues in the world.

The whole area is a feast for the eyes. You can find feng shui gardens up the mountain and a colorful monastery that looks like a palace – with every step you will discover another exciting detail. The most surprising thing I found while I was walking around the giant Buddha was the iron fence at the back of the statue, which allows you a view into the chambers beneath the Buddha. As I looked through, I could see some little lights aglow, like candles on an altar. A little while later, I discovered you could visit the underground section beneath the Buddha - so I did. The experience took my breath away! I have tried to capture the design of that fence into this pincushion. Japan is a country full of small details, just like a pin cushion can be a little but very interesting detail on your desk among your crafting materials.

THERE IS NO OTHER
COUNTRY ON OUR PLANET
WHERE YOU CAN FIND SO
MUCH DIVERSITY AND
CULTURE

PATTERN

With Color A and crochet hook size 1.75mm (4/0), make a ML.

R1 (RS): ch2 (first hdc), make 11hdc more in the loop. Ss in top of first st to connect. Put Color A aside. [12hdc]

R2: Take Color B and attach in blo of any st. Ch1 (doesn't count as st here and throughout entire pattern), (2sc in blo, ch2, 1sc in blo) 4 times. Ss in top of first st to connect. Put Color B aside. [4 sides of 3sc and 4 x ch2-crn]

R3: Pick up Color A in blo of second st on the nearest side. Ch1, *1dc in flo, 1sc in blo, 1sc in the first ch of ch2-crn, ch2, 1sc in the second ch from ch2-crn, 1sc in blo. Rep from * 3 more times. Ss in top of first st to connect. Put Color A aside. [4 sides of 4sc/1dc and 4 x ch2-crn]

R4: Pick up Color B in blo of third st on the nearest side. (this will be a dc). Ch1, *3sc in blo, 1sc in the first ch of ch2-crn, ch2, 1sc in the second ch of ch2-crn, 2sc in blo. Rep from * 3 more times. Ss in top of first st to connect. Put Color B aside. [4 sides of 7sc and 4 x ch2-crn]

R5: Pick up Color A in blo of fourth st on the nearest side. Ch1, *1dc in flo, 3sc in blo, 1sc in the first ch of ch2-crn, ch2, 1sc in the second ch of ch2-crn, 3sc in blo. Rep from * 3 more times. Ss in top of first st to connect. Put Color A aside. [4 sides of 8sc/1dc and 4 x ch2-crn]

R6: Pick up Color B in blo of fifth st on the nearest side. Ch1, *3sc in blo, 1dc in flo, 1sc in blo, 1sc in the first ch of ch2-crn, ch2, 1sc in the second ch of ch2-crn, 1sc in blo, 1dc in flo, 2sc in blo. Rep from * 3 more times. Ss in top of first st to connect. Fasten off Color B. [4 sides of 9sc/2dc and 4 x ch2-crn]

R7: Pick up Color A in blo of sixth st on the nearest side. Ch1, *1dc in flo, 1sc in blo, 1dc in flo, 3sc in blo, 1sc in the first ch of ch2-crn, ch2, 1sc in the second ch of ch2-crn, 3sc in blo, 1dc in flo, 1sc in blo. Rep from * 3 more times. Ss in top of first st to connect. Put Color A aside. [4 sides of 10sc/3dc and 4 x ch2-crn]

R8: Take Color C and attach in blo of seventh st on the nearest side. Ch1, *5sc in blo, 1dc in flo, 1sc in blo, 1sc in the first ch of ch2-crn, ch2, 1sc in the second ch of ch2-crn, 1sc in blo, 1dc in flo, 4sc in blo. Rep from * 3 more times. Ss in top of first st to connect. Put Color C aside. [4 sides of 13sc/2dc and 4 x ch2-crn]

HOOK SIZE NEEDED: 1.75MM (4/0) HOOK

YARN NEEDED: SCHEEPJES MAXI SWEET TREAT COMES IN BALLS OF 25G (1OZ) WITH A LENGTH OF 140M (153YDS) OF YARN. THE YARN CONSISTS OF 100% MERCERIZED COTTON.

- 1 BALL OF SCHEEPJES MAXI SWEET TREAT 110 BLACK (COLOR A)
- 1 BALL OF SCHEEPJES MAXI SWEET TREAT 390 POPPY ROSE (COLOR B)
- 1 BALL OF SCHEEPJES MAXI SWEET TREAT 115 HOT RED (COLOR C)
- 1 BALL OF SCHEEPJES MAXI SWEET TREAT 517 RUBY (COLOR D)

OTHER MATERIALS NEEDED:
10-15G (⅓-½OZ) FIBERFILL
- ONE SMALL METAL BUTTON OF CHOICE (WITH A DIAMETER OF APPROX. 8MM (¼IN)

R9: Pick up Color A in blo of eighth st on the nearest side. Ch1, *(1dc in flo, 3sc in blo) twice, 1sc in the first ch of ch2-crn, ch2, 1sc in the second ch of ch2-crn, 3sc in blo, 1dc in flo, 3sc in blo. Rep from * 3 more times. Ss in top of first st to connect. Put Color A aside. [4 sides of 14sc/3dc and 4 x ch2-crn]

R10: Pick up Color C in blo of ninth st on the nearest side. Ch1, *(3sc in blo, 1dc in flo) twice, 1sc in blo, 1sc in the first ch of ch2-crn, ch2, 1sc in the second ch of ch2-crn, 1sc in blo, 1dc in flo, 3sc in blo, 1dc in flo, 2sc in blo. Rep from * 3 more times. Ss in top of first st to connect. Put Color C aside. [4 sides of 15sc/4dc and 4 x ch2-crn]

R11: Pick up Color A in blo of tenth st on the nearest side. Ch1, *(1dc in flo, 1sc in blo) 4 times, 2sc in blo, 1sc in the first ch of ch2-crn, ch2, 1sc in the second ch of ch2-crn, 3sc in blo, (1dc in flo, 1sc in blo) 3 times. Rep from * 3 more times. Ss in top of first st to connect. Put Color A aside. [4 sides of 14sc/7dc and 4 x ch2-crn]

R12: Pick up Color C in blo of eleventh st on the nearest side. Ch1, *3sc in blo, (1dc in flo, 3sc in blo) twice, 1sc in the first ch of ch2-crn, ch2, 1sc in the second ch of ch2-crn, (3sc in blo, 1dc in flo) twice, 2sc in blo. Rep from * 3 more times. Ss in top of first st to connect. Fasten off Color C. [4 sides of 19sc/4dc and 4 times ch2-crn]

SIZE OF PROJECT: THE PINCUSHION SIZE WILL BE APPROX. 10CM (4IN) FROM SIDE TO SIDE.

TIPS FOR THIS PATTERN:

- THIS PATTERN IS MADE USING THE MOSAIC TECHNIQUE. FOR THIS PATTERN, WE WORK ALL SC STITCHES IN THE BACK LOOP OF THE STS - EXCEPT THE CORNER STS YOU MAKE IN THE CHS.
- IN THE PATTERN, YOU MAKE DC STITCHES IN THE FRONT LOOP OF THE STITCH TWO ROUNDS DOWN. IF YOU MAKE A DC IN R4, YOU WILL USE THE FLO OF THE ST UNDER IT IN R2. YOU ALWAYS SKIP A ST ON THE CURRENT ROUND WHEN MAKING A DC. I HAVE NOT WRITTEN THIS IN THE INSTRUCTIONS, SO KEEP THIS IN MIND.
- THE PATTERN IS WORKED IN THE ROUND. YOU WORK ON THE RIGHT SIDE OF THE PATTERN AT ALL TIMES.
- WHEN PICKING UP A COLOR, ALWAYS DO THAT IN THE BACK LOOP OF THE INDICATED ST.
- WHEN CONNECTING A ROUND WITH AN SS, MAKE A SS THROUGH THE FULL ST.
- WHEN THE PATTERN TELLS YOU TO MAKE 2SC IN BLO, YOU CROCHET 1SC IN BLO OF THE NEXT TWO STS. THE SAME GOES FOR DC STITCHES. THE PATTERN TELLS YOU TO MAKE A DC IN FLO. IN THIS CASE, YOU WILL CROCHET 1 DC IN THE FLO OF THE ST UNDER IT TWO ROWS DOWN.
- IN THE PATTERN, YOU ALWAYS MAKE THE FIRST ST OF THE ROUND IN THE JOINING ST.
- THE DIAGRAM SHOWS ONLY ONE QUARTER OF THE PATTERN. YOU CAN EASILY READ THIS BY STARTING IN THE MIDDLE POINT, WORKING THE RIGHT SIDE AFTER THE MIDDLE POINT, AND THEN WORKING THE LEFT SIDE OF THE SAME ROW.

R13: Pick up Color A in blo of twelfth st on the nearest side. Ch1, *(1dc in flo, 1sc in blo) 4 times, 4sc in blo, 1sc in first ch of ch2-crn, ch2, 1sc in second ch of ch2-crn, 5sc in blo, (1dc in flo, 1sc in blo) 3 times. Rep from * 3 more times. Ss in top of first st to connect. Put Color A aside. [4 sides of 18sc/7dc and 4 x ch2-crn]

R14: Take Color D and attach in blo in thirteenth st on the nearest side. Ch1, *3sc in blo, (1dc in flo, 3sc in blo) twice, 2sc in blo, 1sc in the first ch of ch2-crn, ch2, 1sc in the second ch of ch2-crn, 2sc in blo, (3sc in blo, 1dc in flo) twice, 2sc in blo. Rep from * 3 more times. Ss in top of first st to connect. Put Color D aside. [4 sides of 23sc/4dc and 4 x ch2-crn]

R15: Pick up Color A in blo of fourteenth st on the nearest side. Ch1, *(1dc in flo, 3sc in blo) twice, 6sc in blo, 1sc in the first ch of ch2-crn, ch2, 1sc in the second ch of ch2-crn, 9sc in blo, 1dc in flo, 3sc in blo. Rep from * 3 more times. Ss in top of first st to connect. Put Color A aside. [4 sides of 26sc/3dc and 4 x ch2-crn]

THERE IS A SMALL TOWN BY THE SEASIDE NAMED KAMAKURA

R16: Pick up Color D in blo of fifteenth st on the nearest side. Ch1, *5sc in blo, 1dc in flo, 9sc in blo, 1sc in the first ch of ch2-crn, ch2, 1sc in the second ch of ch2-crn, 9sc in blo, 1dc in flo, 4sc in blo. Rep from * 3 more times. Ss in top of first st to connect. Put Color D aside. [4 sides of 29sc/ 2dc and 4 x ch2-crn]

R17: Pick up Color A in blo of sixteenth st on the nearest side. Ch1, *(1dc in flo, 1sc in blo) twice, 12sc in blo, 1sc in the first ch of ch2-crn, ch2, 1sc in the second ch of ch2-crn, 13sc in blo, 1dc in flo, 1sc in blo. Rep from * 3 more times. Ss in top of first st to connect. Put Color A aside. [4 sides of 30sc/3dc and 4 x ch2-crn]

R18: Pick up Color D in blo of seventeenth st on the nearest side. Ch1, *3sc in blo, 1dc in flo, 13sc in blo, 1sc in the first ch of ch2-crn, ch2, 1sc in the second ch of ch2-crn, 13sc in blo, 1dc in flo, 2sc in blo. Ss in top of first st to connect. Rep from * 3 more times. Fasten off Color D. [4 sides of 33sc/2dc and 4 x ch2-crn]

R19: Pick up Color A in blo of eighteenth st on the nearest side. Ch1, *1dc in flo, 17sc in blo, 1sc in the first ch of ch2-crn, ch2, 1sc in the second ch of ch2-crn, 17sc in blo. Rep from * 3 more times. Ss in top of first st to connect. Fasten off Color A. [4 sides of 36sc/1dc and 4 x ch2-crn]

Weave in all ends and make another similar square by crocheting R1-19 again.

Lay both squares on top of each other, so the RS is facing you. Attach Color A through both ch2-crns and make 2sc. Now, crochet 1ss through each st on both sides at the same time to connect the squares. Repeat this process until you have three sides closed. Take the fiberfill and put it inside the connected squares.
Make sure you stuff it tightly, especially at the corners. Close the last side of the pincushion. Weave in the remaining ends. Put the metal button on a thread and sew it through the top square's middle to the back. Pull the thread at the back of the work tight so the button will sink into the pincushion. Weave in this last thread at the back of the work.

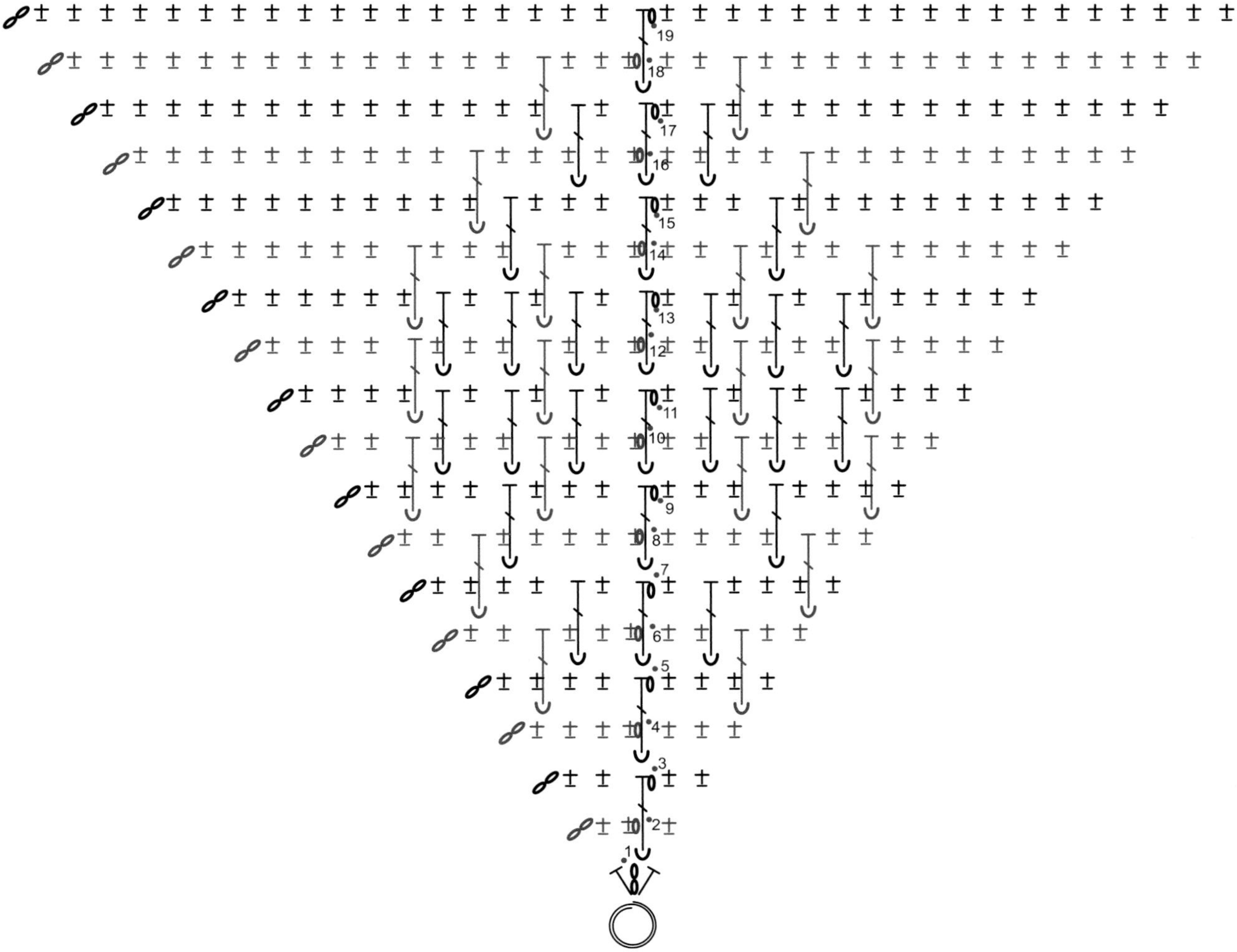

19
18
17
16
15
14
13
12
11
10
9
8
7
6
5
4
3
2
1

37°2'N, 27°25'E
• HARBOR TOWN • GULF OF GÖKOVA
• BEACH • MOSQUES • ST. PETER'S CASTLE

TURKEY (BODRUM)

NAZAR MANDALA

For my very first vacation I wanted to enjoy some sun, sea, and sand so I went to Bodrum, which lies on the west coast of Turkey. It is a common tourist area for those who like to rest and enjoy the summer sun. The whole experience of flying for the first time and entering a new country was so exciting. It leaves a memory for the rest of your life, as these are the first steps you take as a new world traveler. With zero experience and an open mind, I explored Bodrum and the region around it.

Even though this trip gave me my very first souvenir, looking back it also was perhaps a slightly risky thing to do. It was afternoon, the sun was burning on my shoulders, and I had visited the local market of Bodrum. I was walking to a taxi rank to get me back to the resort and, suddenly, a woman started yelling at me from her back garden. As I couldn't understand the Turkish language, I wasn't quite sure how to react. With her body language she indicated that I should go into her garden, and without thinking it through, I opened the fence and just stepped in. With a few words, some bad English, and our body language, we were able to understand each other.

She offered me some Turkish tea and when I got up to leave, she stepped into her house and told me to wait. She came back with a small blue amulet. She gave it to me and told me to keep it. I thanked her with all my heart and went back to the taxi rank.

I discovered later on that she had given me a Nazar amulet. It is known as the blue evil eye, which in some cultures stands for evil and negativity, which can befall you once you receive the amulet. In other cultures it is seen to provide a protection against evil. In Turkey, the blue eye is almost a national gift. I see this first souvenir from my traveling as a token of kindness. Giving it without receiving and wishing the best to someone. The blue eye is a simple amulet with real vivid blue colors, and I tried to capture it by crocheting it with some creative additions.

PATTERN

With crochet hook size 5.0mm (H/8) and Color A, make a ML.

R1 (RS): Ch3 (first dc), make 11dc more in the loop. Ss in top of first st to connect. [12dc]

R2: Ch4 (first dc + ch1), (1dc in next st, ch1) 11 times. Ss in third ch to connect. Ss to next ch1-sp. [12dc /12 x ch1-sp]

R3: Ch1 (doesn't count as st here and throughout entire pattern), (3sc in ch1-sp, sk next st) 12 times. Ss in blo of first st to connect. [36sc]

R4: *Starting in the blo of first st of last Round.* Ch3 (first dc), 1dc in blo of each st on Round. Ss in top of first st to connect. Fasten off Color A. [36dc in blo]

R5: Take Color B and attach in any st on Round. Ch1, (1sc in st, 1tr in flo of next st on Round 3, sk st on current Round) 18 times. Ss in blo of first st to connect. [18sc/18tr in flo]

R6: *Starting in the blo of first st of last Round.* Ch3 (first dc), 1dc in blo of same st, 1dc in blo next st, (2dc in blo of next st, 1dc in blo of next st) 17 times. Ss in top of first st to connect. Fasten off Color B. [54dc in blo]

R7: Take Color C and attach in a single dc on Round. So, not a dc in the 2dc-increases of the last Round, but a dc between those. Ch1, *1sc in next 2 sts, 1fpdtr around the tr of Round 5 you just passed *(this is not the one which lies ahead, but the one you have just crocheted over)*, sk st on current Round *(the skipped st will be a second dc out a 2dc-increase of last Round)*. Rep from * 17 more times. Ss in blo of first st to connect. [36sc/18fpdtr]

R8: *Starting in the blo of first st of last Round, which will be the first sc out of two between two fpdtr stitches.* Ch2 (first hdc), 1hdc in blo of next st, 2hdc in blo of next st *(this will be an fpdtr)*, (1hdc in blo of next 2 sts, 2hdc in blo of next st) 17 times. Ss in top of first st to connect. Fasten off Color C. [72hdc in blo]

R9: Take Color D and attach in any hdc, which is made **<u>after</u>** a 2hdc-increase. Ch1, * 1sc in next 3 sts, 1fpdtr around the fpdtr of Round 7 you just passed *(this is not the one which lies ahead, but the one you have just crocheted over)*, sk st on current Round *(which will be a second hdc out of a 2hdc-increase of last Round)*. Rep from * 17 more times. Ss in blo of first st to connect. [54sc/18fpdtr]

R10: *Starting in blo of first st of last Round, an sc after an fpdtr.* Ch2 (first hdc), 1hdc in blo of same st, 1hdc in blo of next 3 sts, (2hdc in blo of next st, 1hdc in blo of next

<u>HOOK SIZE NEEDED:</u> 5.0MM (H/8) HOOK

<u>YARN NEEDED:</u> SCHEEPJES CAHLISTA COMES IN BALLS OF 50G (1¾OZ) WITH A LENGTH OF 85M (93YDS) OF YARN. THE YARN CONSISTS OF 100% NATURAL COTTON.

- 1 BALL OF SCHEEPJES CAHLISTA – COLOR 110 JET BLACK (COLOR A)
- 1 BALL OF SCHEEPJES CAHLISTA – COLOR 146 VIVID BLUE (COLOR B)
- 1 BALL OF SCHEEPJES CAHLISTA – COLOR 510 SKY BLUE (COLOR C)
- 1 BALL OF SCHEEPJES CAHLISTA – COLOR 509 BABY BLUE (COLOR D)
- 1 BALL OF SCHEEPJES CAHLISTA – COLOR 106 SNOW WHITE (COLOR E)
- 1 BALL OF SCHEEPJES CAHLISTA – COLOR 247 BLUEBIRD (COLOR F)
- 1 BALL OF SCHEEPJES CAHLISTA – COLOR 201 ELECTRIC BLUE (COLOR G)

3 sts) 17 times. Ss in top of first st to connect. Fasten off Color D. [90hdc in blo]

R11: Take Color E and attach in any second hdc in of a 2hdc-increase of last Round. Ch1, *1sc in st, 1fptr around fpdtr of Round 9 which lies ahead of you, sk st on current Round, 1sc in next 3 sts. Rep from * 17 more times. Ss in top of first st to connect. [72sc/18fptr]

R12: *Starting in first st of last Round, which will be an sc before an fptr.* Ch2 (first hdc), 1pc around next fptr of Round 11, sk st on current Round, 1hdc in next 2 sts, 2hdc in next st. *1hdc in next st, 1pc around the fptr of Round 11, sk st on current Round, 1hdc in next 2 sts, 2hdc in next st. Rep from * 16 more times. Ss in top of first st to connect. Ss to next pc st. [90hdc/18pc]

R13: *Starting in pc st.* Ch6 (first dc + ch3), sk 2 sts, (1dc in next st, ch3, sk next 2 sts) 35 times. Ss in the third ch to connect. Fasten off Color E. [36dc/ 36 x ch3-sp]

R14: Take Color F and attach in any ch3-sp. Ch3 (first dc), 3dc in same ch3-sp, sk next st, (4dc in next ch3-sp, sk next st) 35 times. Ss in top of first st to connect. [144dc]

R15: Ch2 (no st, only made to get to the back of your work), 1bphdc around each st on Round. Ss in blo of first st to connect. [144bphdc]

R16: Ch3 (first dc), 1dc in blo of each st on Round. Ss in top of first st to connect. Fasten off Color F. [144dc in blo]

- 1 BALL OF SCHEEPJES CAHLISTA – COLOR 527 MIDNIGHT (COLOR H)

OTHER MATERIALS NEEDED:
OPTIONAL; METAL RING WITH A DIAMETER OF 50CM (20IN) TO HOLD THE MANDALA.

SIZE OF PROJECT: THE DIAMETER OF THE MANDALA WILL BE APPROX. 50CM (20IN).

TIPS FOR THIS PATTERN:

- WHEN MAKING FRONT POST STITCHES IN THE PATTERN, YOU ALWAYS SKIP A STITCH ON THE CURRENT ROUND BEHIND THE FRONT POST STITCH.
- YOU CAN CROCHET THIS MANDALA INTO A RING, BUT IT IS OPTIONAL.
- IN THIS PATTERN, WE WORK IN ROUNDS. WE CROCHET AT THE RIGHT SIDE OF THE WORK FOR THE ENTIRE PATTERN.
- IN THIS PATTERN, YOU WILL WORK STS IN THE FRONT LOOP OF PREVIOUS ROUNDS. ALWAYS MAKE THE ST IN THE FRONT LOOP UNDERNEATH THE CURRENT STITCH AND SKIP A ST ON THE CURRENT ROUND.
- BECAUSE I AM LEFT-HANDED, THE FINISHED RESULT IN THE BOOK MIGHT SHOW A MIRRORED VIEW. THE OUTCOME OF A RIGHT-HANDED CROCHETER MIGHT BE THE OPPOSITE. IN THIS PARTICULAR PATTERN, YOU WILL NOTICE IT DUE TO THE PATTERN'S SKEWED LINES AND TEXTURE.
- THE FIRST ST ON A ROUND WILL ALWAYS BE MADE IN THE STITCH OF ATTACHMENT.

R17: Take Color G and attach in any st on Round. Ch1, (1sc in next 5 sts, 1tr in flo of following st on Round 15, sk st on current Round) 24 times. Ss in blo of first st to connect. [120sc/24tr]

R18: *Starting in blo of first st of last Round, an sc after a tr.* Ch3 (first dc), 1dc in blo of next 4 sts, 2dc in blo of next st (which will be a tr), (1dc in blo of next 5 sts, 2dc in blo of next st) 23 times. Ss in top of first st to connect. Fasten off Color G. [168dc in blo]

R19: Take Color H and attach in any second dc of a 2dc-increase of last Round. Ch1, *1sc in next 3 sts, 1tr in flo of next st on Round 17 *(which will be the middle flo of a set of 5 dc in Round 17)*, sk st on current Round, 1sc in next 2 sts, 1fptr around next tr of Round 17, sk st on current Round. Rep from * 23 more times. Ss in blo of first st to connect. [120sc/24tr/24fptr]

R20: *Starting in blo of first st on last Round, which will be an sc after an fptr.* Ch3 (first dc), 1dc in blo of each st on Round. Ss in top of first st to connect. [168dc in blo]

R21: *Starting in first st of last Round.* Ch1, *1sc in next 2 sts, 1fptr around next tr of Round 19, sk st on current Round, 2sc in next st, 1sc in next st, 1fptr around next fptr of Round 19, sk st on current Round, 1sc in next st. Rep from * 23 more times. Ss in blo of first st to connect. [144sc/48fptr]

R22: *Starting in blo of first st of last Round, which will be the second sc after the previous fptr you made around an fptr of Round 19.* Ch2 (first hdc), 1hdc in blo of next st, 2hdc in blo of next st *(this will be an fptr you made around a tr on Round 19)*, 1hdc in blo of next 5 sts. *1hdc in blo of next 2 sts, 2hdc in blo of next st, 1hdc in blo of next 5 sts. Rep from * 22 more times. Ss in top of first st to connect. Fasten off Color H. [216hdc in blo]

R23: Take Color G and attach in any first hdc of a 2hdc-increase. Ch1, *1sc in next 4 sts, 1fpdtr around next fptr of Round 21, sk st on current Round, 1sc in next 3 sts, 1fpdtr around next fptr of Round 21, sk st on current Round. Rep from * 23 more times. Ss in top of first st to connect. Fasten off Color G. [168sc/48fpdtr]

R24: Take Color F and attach in any first sc out of three between two fpdtr stitches. Ch1, *1sc in next 3 sts, 1puff around next fpdtr of Round 23, sk st on current Round, 1sc in next 4 sts, 1puff around next fpdtr of Round 23, sk st on current Round. Rep from * 23 more times. Ss in top of first st to connect. Fasten off Color F. [168sc/48puff sts]

R25: Take Color D and attach in any puff st **before** 4 sc. Ch1, *(1sc in next 6 sts, 2sc in next st, 1sc in next 2 sts) 24 times. Ss in top of first st to connect. Fasten off Color D. [240sc]

R26: Take Color C and attach in any st on Round. Ch3 (first hdc + ch1), sk next st, (1hdc in next st, ch1, sk next st) 119 times. Ss in the second ch to connect. Fasten off Color C. [120hdc/120 x ch1-sp]

It is time to take your ring and attach the mandala into the ring in the next Round. You will crochet the 3sc stitches around the ring and the ch1-sps at the same time to get it attached to the ring. If you didn't want to use a circle, then make the 3sc stitches in the ch1-sp just as you usually would do.

R27: Take Color B and attach in any ch1-sp. Ch1, (3sc in ch1-sp, sk next st) 120 times. Ss in top of first st to connect. Fasten off Color B. [120 gr of 3sc]

Weave in all ends and if you didn't use a ring, block the project into a circle for the best outcome.

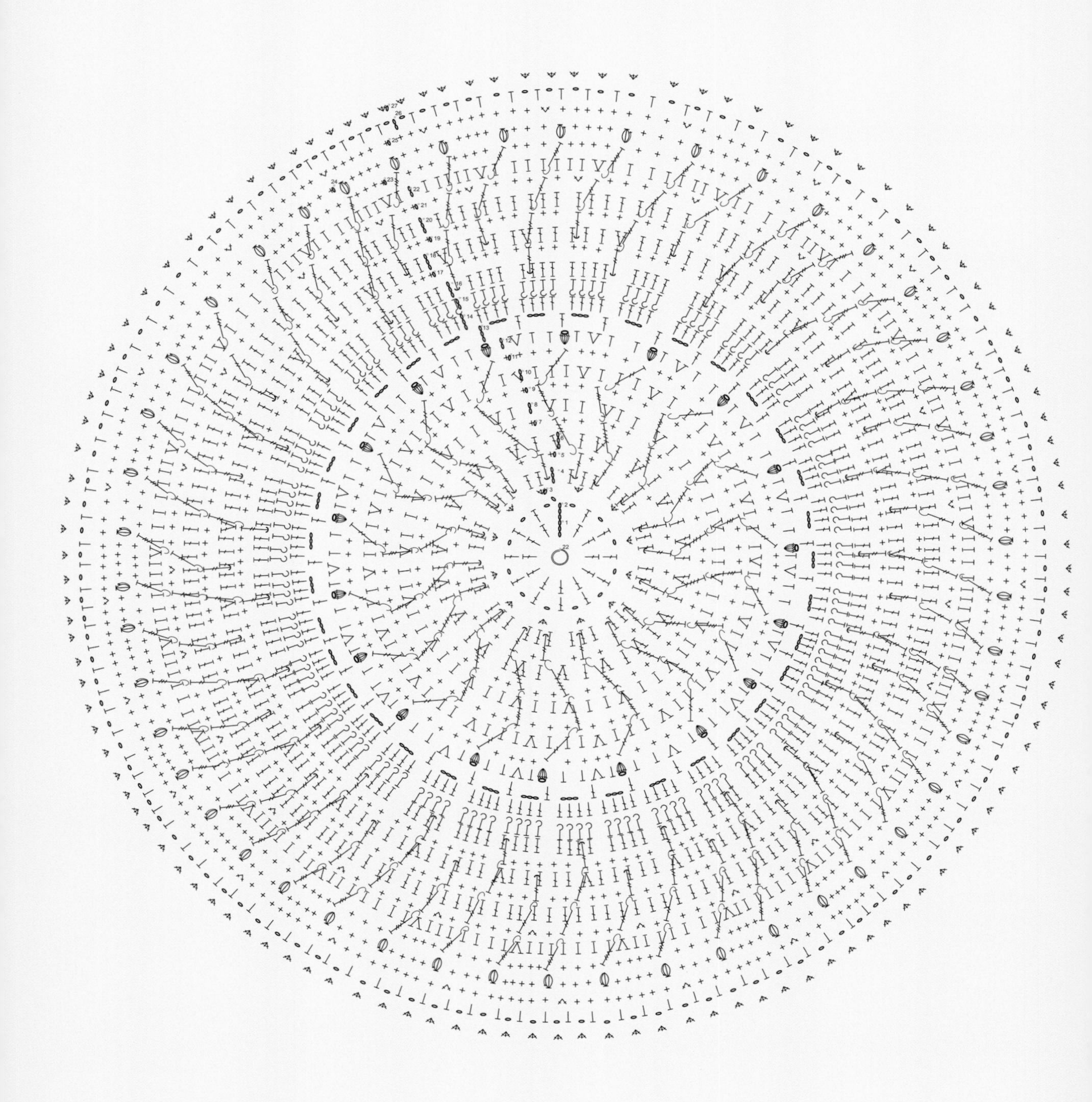

SHE CAME BACK WITH
A SMALL BLUE
AMULET IN HER HAND

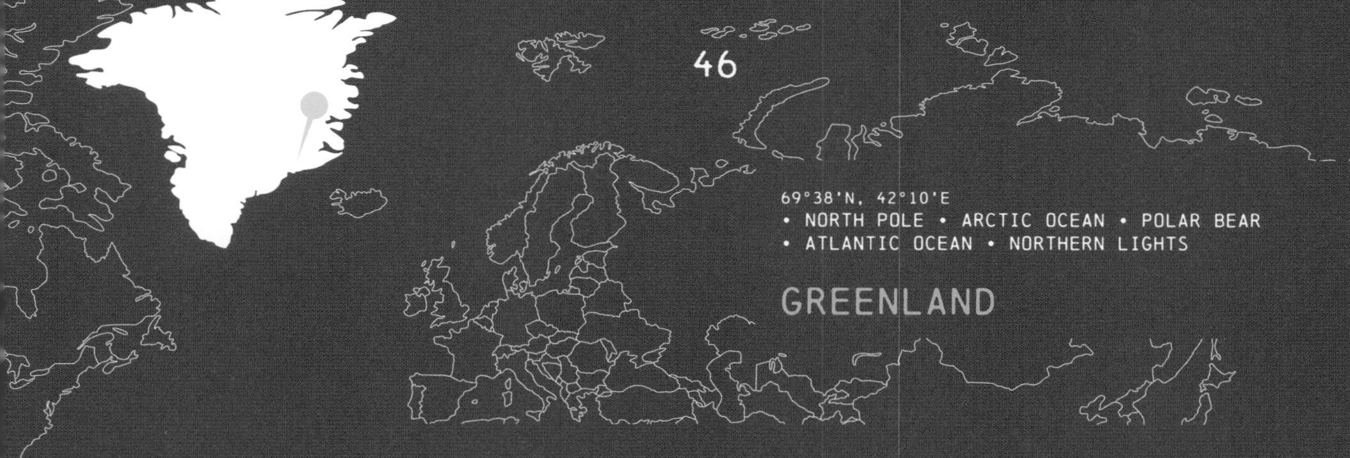

FADING LIGHT SCARF

One of the most memorable trips I've had must be the one to the North. I booked a flight to Iceland, where I traveled through the countryside and volcanic grounds. I visited waterfalls and geysers and also experienced snowstorms and temperatures below zero. After a week of traveling through Iceland, it was time to move on. I rented a boat to take me up to the coast of Greenland. There is only a small ocean to cross between Greenland and Iceland so the journey wouldn't be that long. However, the night before we were due to leave, a storm began. It was touch and go whether we would be able to carry on, and as a precaution I took some sea sickness pills and put on an "astronaut" suit to keep out the freezing winds. Finally, we had the green light to leave, and endured a bumpy three-hour ride on the wild ocean. At least we had the company of some whales who swam with us in the direction of Greenland! After what seemed like a long time, we reached the port.

Greenland felt like the end of the world but traveling there would end up being an experience to treasure for life. I did several hikes around Greenland during my time there, but the most amazing one was at night - standing on a plain of ice watching the sky, hoping to spot those green lights (better known as the Northern Lights). I had the good fortune to see this magical gift of nature with my own eyes. It makes you feel so small and insignificant standing there with a spectrum of colors above you in the dark night. It was an experience that I couldn't leave out of this book. As the Northern Lights are such an explosion of color, I focused on colorwork in this pattern.

PATTERN

With hook size 5.5mm (I/9) and Color A, ch62.

R1 (WS): Make a sc in the second ch from the hook. Make a sc in each ch of Row. Turn work. [61sc]

R2 (RS): Ch3 (first dc), sk next 2 sts, (2dc-ch1-2dc in next st, sk next 5 sts) 9 times. 2dc-ch1-1dc in next st, sk next 2 sts, 1dc in last st of Row. Fasten off Color A. Turn work. [10 gr of 2dc-ch1-2dc and 2dc on the sides]

R3 (WS): Take Color B and attach in first st on Row at the Wrong Side of the work. (This will be the last made st in the previous Row). Ch1 (doesn't count as st here and throughout entire pattern), 1sc in first st of Row, 1ext. dc in first sk st out of 2 skipped sts on last Row (that is into the Row 1 st), ch1, sk next 2dc on current Row, 1sc in next ch1-sp which lies between the two 2dc-gr, ch1, sk next 2dc on current Row. *1ext. dc-ch1-1 ext. dc in third skipped st of next 5 sk sts on last Row *(this will be the middle sk st from Row 1)*, ch1, sk next 2dc on current Row, 1sc in next ch1-sp between

Special stitches in the pattern:
Extended dc (ext. dc): In the pattern, you will crochet an extended dc. You will work this stitch over earlier-made stitches. Here is how to make the extended dc:

- Yarn over hook, just as you would do with a regular dc.
- Insert crochet hook in the indicated ch-sp and pull up a second loop through this ch-sp. Pull this as far as possible up until you reach the level of the Row you are currently working on. You will pull up this loop over all existing stitches.
- Now, finish the dc as you would normally.

HOOK SIZE NEEDED: 5.5MM (I/9) HOOK

YARN NEEDED: SCHEEPJES MERINO SOFT COMES IN BALLS OF 50G (1¾OZ) WITH A LENGTH OF 105M (114YDS) OF YARN. THE YARN CONSISTS OF 50% SUPERWASH MERINO/25% MICROFIBER/25% ACRYLIC.

- 1 BALL SCHEEPJES MERINO SOFT – COLOR 618 WOOD (COLOR A)
- 1 BALL SCHEEPJES MERINO SOFT – COLOR 655 CHAGALL (COLOR B)
- 1 BALL SCHEEPJES MERINO SOFT – COLOR 637 SEURAT (COLOR C)
- 1 BALL SCHEEPJES MERINO SOFT – COLOR 639 MONET (COLOR D)
- 1 BALL SCHEEPJES MERINO SOFT – COLOR 654 BELLINI (COLOR E)
- 1 BALL SCHEEPJES MERINO SOFT – COLOR 600 MALEVICH (COLOR F)
- 1 BALL SCHEEPJES MERINO SOFT – COLOR 651 PISSARRO (COLOR G)
- 1 BALL SCHEEPJES MERINO SOFT – COLOR 628 BOTTICELLI (COLOR H)
- 1 BALL SCHEEPJES MERINO SOFT – COLOR 625 KANDINSKY (COLOR I)

2dc-gr, ch1, sk next 2dc on current Row. Rep from * 8 more times. 1 ext. dc in second sk st out of 2 sk sts on last Row (into the Row 1 st), 1sc in last st of Row *(this will be the ch3 with which you started in the last Row)*. Turn work. [2 individual ext. dc/ 9 gr of 1 ext.dc–ch1–1 ext. dc and 12sc with 20 ch1-sps between them]

R4 (RS): Ch3 (first dc), make 2dc more in same st, (sk every st until next ch1-sp between 2 ext. dc stitches, 2dc-ch1-2dc in next ch1-sp) 9 times. Sk all sts to last st on Row, 3dc in last st of Row. Fasten off Color B. Turn work. [9 gr of 2dc-ch1-2dc and 2 gr of 3dc on the sides]

R5 (WS): Take Color C and attach in first st on Row at the Wrong Side of the work. (This will be the last made st of the previous Row). Ch1, 1sc in first st of Row, *ch1, sk next 2dc on previous Row, 1ext. dc–ch1–1ext. dc in ch1-sp between two 2dc-gr on Row 2 – you also made a sc in this ch1-sp already *(and you will work the ext. dc over the sc)*, ch1, sk next 2dc on current Row, 1sc in next ch1-sp between two 2dc-gr on previous Row. Rep from * 8 more times. Ch1, sk next 2dc on current Row, 1ext. dc–ch1–1ext. dc in next ch1-sp between two 2dc-gr on Row 2, ch1, sk next 2dc on previous Row, 1sc in last st of Row. Turn work. [10 gr of ext. dc–ch1–ext. dc and 11sc with 20 ch1-sps]

- 1 BALL SCHEEPJES MERINO SOFT – COLOR 630 LAUTREC (COLOR J)

SIZE: THE LENGTH OF THE SCARF WILL BE ABOUT 160–175CM (63–69IN). THE WIDTH OF THE SCARF WILL BE ABOUT 30CM (12IN).

TIPS FOR THIS PATTERN:

- FOR THIS PATTERN, I USED A LOT OF COLORS. YOU WILL HAVE A LOT OF ENDS TO WEAVE IN. OF COURSE, IT IS POSSIBLE TO MAKE THIS PATTERN WITH JUST ONE COLOR OR A GRADIENT TYPE OF YARN. YOU CAN IGNORE THE ATTACHING AND FASTENING OFF DURING THE ROWS IF YOU MAKE THIS CHOICE. IT WILL REDUCE THE NUMBER OF ENDS TO WEAVE IN DRAMATICALLY.
- THE PATTERN IS CROCHETED WITH A COMBINATION OF STITCHES, WHICH WILL DELIVER A TIGHT TENSION. IT IS ESSENTIAL TO GO UP AT LEAST ONE HOOK SIZE MORE THAN THE ADVISED SIZE FOR THE YARN YOU WILL USE. BY DOING THIS, YOUR SCARF WILL BECOME MORE COMFORTABLE TO WEAR.
- THE SCARF CAN BE ADJUSTED IN LENGTH – FOR THIS, YOU ADD OR REMOVE REPEAT ROWS TO THE PATTERN. FOR WIDTH, YOU CAN ADD OR REMOVE 6 STITCHES FOR EACH REPEAT. WHEN DOING THIS, YOU WILL ALSO NEED TO ADJUST THE NUMBER OF REPEATS IN A ROW.
- THE PATTERN IS CROCHETED IN ROWS, WHICH MEANS YOU WILL WORK ON THE RIGHT SIDE OF THE WORK AND THE WRONG SIDE OF THE WORK.
- IN THE FIRST ROWS, YOUR PATTERN CAN LOOK A BIT OUT OF BALANCE AS IT MIGHT CURL A LITTLE OR GET OUT OF SHAPE. IT WILL FALL IN PLACE AFTER CROCHETING FURTHER ROWS AND THE PATTERN DEVELOPS.
- FOR A NEATER CHANGE OF COLORS, YOU CAN PULL A NEW COLOR THROUGH THE LOOPS OF THE LAST ST ON A ROW WHERE YOU NEED TO FASTEN OFF THE YARN AND ATTACH A NEW COLOR.

R6 (RS): Ch3 (first dc), (sk all sts until next ch1-sp between 2 ext. dc stitches, 2dc-ch1-2dc in next ch1-sp) 10 times. Sk all sts till last st of Row. 1dc in last st of Row. Fasten off Color C. Turn work. [2dc and 10 gr of 2dc-ch1-2dc]

R7 (WS): Take Color D and attach in first st of Row at the Wrong Side of the work. (This will be the last st made on the previous Row). Ch1, 1sc in first st of Row, 1ext. dc in the second dc out of the 3dc-gr on Row 4, *ch1, sk next 2dc on previous Row, 1sc in next ch1-sp between two 2dc-gr, ch1, sk next 2dc on previous Row, 1ext. dc–ch1–1ext. dc in next ch1-sp between two 2dc-gr on Row 4 where you already made a sc in. Rep from * 8 more times. Sk next 2dc on previous Row, ch1, 1sc in next ch1-sp between two 2dc-gr on previous Row, ch1, sk next 2dc on previous Row, 1ext. dc in the second dc of 3dc-gr on Row 4, 1sc in last of Row. Turn work. [2 individual ext. dc/9 gr of ext. dc–ch1–ext. dc/10sc with 20 ch1-sps and 1sc on both sides]

R8 (RS): Ch3 (first dc), make 2dc more in same st, (sk every st until next ch1-sp between 2 ext. dc stitches, 2dc-ch1-2dc in next ch1-sp) 9 times. Sk all sts until last st on Row, 3dc in last st of Row. Fasten off Color D. Turn work. [9 gr of 2dc-ch1-2dc and 2 gr of 3dc on the sides]

R9 (WS): Take Color E and attach in first st on Row at the Wrong Side of the work. (This will be the last made st of the previous Row). Ch1, 1sc in first st of Row, *ch1, sk next 2dc on previous Row, 1ext. dc-ch1-1ext. dc. dc in ch1-sp between two 2dc-gr which lies three Rows under it – you also made a sc in this ch1-sp already *(and you will work the ext. dc over the sc)*, ch1, sk next 2dc on previous Row, 1sc in next ch1-sp between two 2dc-gr on previous Row. Rep from * 8 more times. Ch1, sk next 2dc on previous Row, 1ext. dc–ch1–1ext. dc in next ch1-sp between two 2dc-gr which lies three Rows under it, ch1, sk next 2dc on previous Row, 1sc in last st of Row. Turn work. [10 gr of ext. dc-ch1-ext. dc and 11sc with 20 ch1-sps]

R10 (RS): Ch3 (first dc), (sk all sts until next ch1-sp between 2 ext. dc stitches, 2dc-ch1-2dc in next ch1-sp) 10 times. Sk all sts until last st of Row. 1dc in last st of Row. Fasten off Color E. Turn work. [2dc and 10 gr of 2dc-ch1-2dc]

R11 (WS): Take Color F and attach in first st of Row at the Wrong Side of the work. (This will be the last st made on the previous Row). Ch1, 1sc in first st of Row, 1ext. dc in the second dc out of the 3dc-gr which lies three Rows under it, *ch1, sk next 2dc on previous Row, 1sc in next ch1-sp between two 2dc-gr, ch1, sk next 2dc on previous Row, 1ext. dc–ch1–1ext. dc in next ch1-sp between two 2dc-gr, which lies three Rows under it and where you already made a sc in. Rep from * 8 more times. Sk next 2dc on current Row, ch1, 1sc in next ch1-sp between two 2dc-gr on previous Row, ch1, sk next 2dc on previous Row, 1ext. dc in the second dc of 3dc-gr, which lies three Rows under it, 1sc in last of Row. Turn work. [2 individual ext. dc/ 9 gr of dc-ch1-ext. dc/10sc with 20 ch1-sps and 1sc on both sides]

R12 (RS): Ch3 (first dc), make 2dc more in same st, (sk every st until next ch1-sp between 2 ext. dc stitches, 2dc-ch1-2dc in next ch1-sp) 9 times. Sk all sts until last st on Row, 3dc in last st of Row. Fasten off Color F. Turn work. [9 gr of 2dc-ch1-2dc and 2 gr of 3dc on the sides]

Keep repeating **Rows 9-12**. After every 2 Rows of pattern, you will fasten off and attach a new color. The order of colors used for the example are: **Color A to J**, and after that, reverse the colors by taking **Color J to A** once again. Keep going in this order. It means only Color A and J will be used twice after each other and result in 4 Rows of repeats. The other colors will still change after every 2 Rows of repeats.

Keep repeating the pattern until you have used most of your yarn up. Keep a small amount to make some tassels later on. Which color you end with isn't that important as long as you end with a Row 11. After you have made a Row 11 as the last Row, turn your work.

Make a ch, crochet 1sc in each st and ch1-sp on the last Row giving 61sc. Fasten off the yarn and weave in all ends before you continue with the tassels.

Attaching tassels to your scarf:
On both ends, I have attached one tassel of each Color yarn used. It gives ten tassels on each end, which I spread out evenly along the edge, with 5 or 6 stitches between each tassel. Make a tassel by cutting 5 or 6 threads approx. 30cm (12 in) in length. Wrap these threads around your fingers. Now lay the yarn on the point where you want to attach the tassel. Pull the yarn with your crochet hook partly through the stitch. Once the yarn is through the stitch, divide the strands equally on both sides. Now make a slipknot by using both sides of the yarn and pull it tight, right up to the attachment point. Once all 10 tassels are attached on an edge, cut them all the same length. If you find making tassels is tricky, you can also check out my website for a full explanation of this process.

IT MAKES YOU FEEL SO SMALL STANDING THERE WITH A SPECTRUM OF COLORS ABOVE YOU IN THE DARK NIGHT

FADING LIGHT SCARF

54

25°19'N, 82°59'E
• THE GANGES • BENARES • PLACE OF PILGRIMAGE • RITUALS • FAITH • COLORS

INDIA (VARANASI)

RITUALS POUF

One of the most exciting countries on our planet is India. The land is full of various different traditions, cultures, and beautiful colors. For that reason alone, it deserves to be featured in this book. I could write a story about the wonder of the Taj Mahal or the famous Red Fort, but I have chosen quite a different focus.

Come with me to the city of Varanasi - a holy place divided by the Ganges river; a city where ancient rituals and beliefs are still strong. If you walk around the town, you will enter the streets around the Ganges where you will find "offering places"; extended arches of stone point into the direction of the river and, on these arches, the bodies of those who have passed away are burned with many offerings and rituals. Once the body turns to ash, the ash is thrown into the river so that the Ganges can carry the person to the afterlife. For a stranger, these rituals may seem unpleasant at first sight.

The smell, noise, and the view will stay with you for a long time but later on, when you think over what you have experienced, you will see the beauty of it. There is serenity in the way people pay a tribute to their loved ones and openly share their grief. I still remember the times I walked along the river, looking into the grey and brown colors of the water, seeing flowers, offerings with lights, and even human remains floating by. You might read this with disgust, but do try to see the raw beauty of it; It makes you realize how death is still a part of life, which is often shut away in the Western world.

On the other hand, India will dazzle you with color, helping to brighten up these dark moments. Walls, flowers, shops, and people show off a myriad of colors. These high contrasts make India a very unique place. For that reason, I came up with the Rituals pouf. The pouf displays the kinds of colors and elements you can find at temples and places around Varanasi.

THE LAND IS FULL
OF TRADITIONS,
CULTURES AND
COLORS

PATTERN

With crochet hook size 5.5mm (I/9) and Color A, make a ML.

R1 (RS): Ch1 (doesn't count as st here and throughout entire pattern), make 6sc in the loop. Ss in top of first st to connect. [6sc]

R2: Ch1, (2sc in st) 6 times. Ss in top of first st to connect. Put Color A aside. [12sc]

R3: Take Color B and attach it in any st on Round. Ch1, (1sc in st, sk next st, ch3) 6 times. Ss in top of first st to connect. Put Color B aside. [6sc/6 x ch3-sp]

R4: Pick up Color A in nearest sc made in previous Round. Ch1, (1sc in sc between two ch3-sps, 1dc-ch1-1dc in next sk st on Round 2 under the ch3-sp *(you will make the dc-ch1-dc* ***in front*** *of the ch3-sp)*) 6 times. Ss in top of first st to connect. Put Color A aside. [6sc/12dc/6 x ch1-sp]

R5: Pick up Color B in nearest sc made on previous Round. Ch5 (1dc + ch2), 1puff st in ch3-sp of Round 3 *(you will pull the ch3-sp of Round 3 through the space between the two dc stitches of Round 4 and make the puff in it)*, ch2, (1dc in next sc, ch2, 1puff st in ch3-sp of Round 3, ch2) 5 times. Ss in the third ch to connect. Put Color B aside. [6dc/6 puff sts/12 x ch2-sp]

R6: Pick up Color A in nearest puff st of previous Round. Ch1, (1sc in puff st, 1fptr around the next dc of Round 4, 2sc in next dc of Round 5, 1fptr around next dc of Round 4) 6 times. Ss in top of first st to connect. Put Color A aside. [18sc/12fptr]

R7: Pick up Color B in nearest first sc of a 2sc-increase of previous Round. Ch1, (1sc in first sc of 2sc-increase, 1sc in next st, 2sc in next st *(which will be an fptr)*, 1sc in next st, 2sc in next st *(which will be the next fptr)*) 6 times. Ss in top of first st to connect. Put Color B aside. [42sc]

R8: Pick up Color A in nearest first sc of a 2sc-increase **before** a puff st. Ch1, (1sc in st, 1sc in next st, 1fpdc2tog around next 2 fptr stitches of Round 6, sk st, 1sc in next 4 sts) 6 times. Ss in top of first st to connect. Put Color A aside. [36sc/6 x fpdc2tog]

R9: Pick up Color B in nearest fpdc2tog of previous Round. Ch1, (1sc in fpdc2tog, 1sc in next 2 sts, 2sc in

HOOK SIZE NEEDED: 5.5MM (I/9) HOOK

YARN NEEDED: SCHEEPJES CHUNKY MONKEY COMES IN BALLS OF 100G (3½OZ) WITH A LENGTH OF 116M (126YDS) OF YARN. THE YARN CONSISTS OF 100% PREMIUM ANTI-PILLING ACRYLIC.

- 3 BALLS OF SCHEEPJES CHUNKY MONKEY – COLOR 1724 HEATHER (COLOR A)
- 1 BALL OF SCHEEPJES CHUNKY MONKEY – COLOR 1117 ROYAL BLUE (COLOR B)
- 1 BALL OF SCHEEPJES CHUNKY MONKEY – COLOR 1435 MAGENTA (COLOR C)
- 1 BALL OF SCHEEPJES CHUNKY MONKEY – COLOR 1709 OCHRE (COLOR D)
- 1 BALL OF SCHEEPJES CHUNKY MONKEY – COLOR 2003 PASSION FRUIT (COLOR E)
- 1 BALL OF SCHEEPJES CHUNKY MONKEY – COLOR 1725 EUCALYPTUS (COLOR F)

OTHER MATERIALS NEEDED: 1 POUF WITH A 38-40CM (15-16IN) DIAMETER AND A HEIGHT OF 15CM (6IN).

SIZE OF PROJECT: THE FINISHED SIZE OF THE POUF WILL BE THE SAME AS THE POUF USED. IF YOU ONLY WANT

TO CROCHET THE CIRCLE FOR THE TOP AND BOTTOM, IT WILL MEASURE APPROXIMATELY 36CM (14IN).

TIPS FOR THIS PATTERN:

- AS WE WORK THIS PATTERN IN ROUNDS, ALL ROUNDS ARE CROCHETED ON THE RIGHT SIDE.
- AS THE PATTERN IS MADE WITH A THICK AND CHUNKY YARN, THE PATTERN WILL BE VERY TIGHT. THE COVER FOR THE POUF SHOULD NOT SHOW ANY GAPS BETWEEN YOUR STITCHES ONCE THE POUF IS INSERTED.
- IF YOU ONLY CROCHET ROUNDS 1-24, YOU WILL HAVE THE CIRCLE FOR THE POUF'S TOP OR BOTTOM. IT WOULD ALSO BE PERFECT TO USE AS A DOILY. IF YOU DECIDE TO DO THIS, I WOULD SUGGEST SIZING UP YOUR CROCHET HOOK BY ONE SIZE TO MAKE THE PATTERN LESS TIGHT.
- THE CHART FOR THIS PATTERN SHOWS THE TOP AND BOTTOM OF THE POUF, THE SIDE IS SHOWN IN ABBREVIATED ROWS SO YOU CAN SEE HOW THE PATTERN WORKS.

next st, 1sc in next 3 sts) 6 times. Ss in top of first st to connect. Fasten off Color B. [48sc]

R10: Pick up Color A in nearest second sc of a 2sc-increase of previous Round. Ch1, (1sc in st, 1sc in next 2 sts, 2sc in next st, 1sc in next st, 2sc in next st, 1sc in next 2 sts) 6 times. Ss in top of first st to connect. Put Color A aside. [60sc]

R11: Take Color C and attach it in any st on Round. Ch1, (1sc in st, ch3, sk next st) 30 times. Ss in top of first st to connect. Put Color C aside. [30sc/30 x ch3-sp]

R12: Pick up Color A in nearest sc made in previous Round. Ch1, (1sc in sc between two ch3-sps, 1dc-ch1-1dc in next sk st on Round 10 under the ch3-sp *(you will make the dc-ch1-dc* ***in front*** *of the ch3-sp)* 30 times. Ss in top of first st to connect. Put Color A aside. [30sc/60dc/30 x ch1-sp]

From this point, the next Rounds can be a bit bobbly or out of shape as the tension of the pattern will get very tight. The problem will sort itself out during the Rounds as the number of stitches will be divided differently.

R13: Pick up Color C in nearest sc made on previous Round. Ch4 (1dc + ch1), 1puff st in ch3-sp of Round 11 *(you will pull the ch3-sp of Round 11 through the space between the two dc stitches of Round 12 and make the puff in it)*, ch1, (1dc in next sc, ch1, 1puff st in ch3-sp of

Round 11 ch1) 29 times. Ss in the third ch to connect. Put Color C aside. [30dc/30 puff sts/60 x ch1-sp]

R14: Pick up Color A in nearest dc made in the previous Round. Ch1, (2sc in dc, 1fptr2tog over both dc stitches of Round 12 – *you will take a dc from both sides of the puff st, in this way, you will enclose the puff st in the fptr2tog)* – 30 times. Ss in top of first st to connect. Put Color A aside. [60sc/30 x fptr2tog]

R15: Pick up Color C in nearest st of previous Round. Ch1, 1sc in each st of Round. Ss in top of first st to connect. Fasten off Color C. [90sc]

R16: Pick up Color A in nearest st, which lies directly above an fptr2tog of Round 14. Ch1, 1fpdc around the fptr2tog of Round 14, sk 1 st, 1sc in next 2 sts, (1fpdc around next fptr2tog of Round 14, sk st, 1sc in next 2 sts) 29 times. Ss in top of first st to connect. Put Color A aside. [60sc/30fpdc]

R17: Take Color D and attach it in any fpdc of the previous Round. Ch1, (1sc in fpdc, 1sc in next st, 2sc in next st) 30 times. Ss in top of first st. Put Color D aside. [120sc]

R18: Pick up Color A in nearest first sc of a 2sc-increase of previous Round. Ch1, (1sc in first sc of 2sc-increase, 1sc in next st, 1puff st around the fpdc of Round 16, sk st, 1sc in next st) 30 times. Ss in top of first st to connect. Put Color A aside. [90sc/30puff sts]

R19: Pick up Color D in nearest st of previous Round. Ch2 (first hdc), 1hdc in each st of Round. Ss in top of first st to connect. Fasten off Color D. [120hdc]

R20: Pick up Color A in nearest st of previous Round. Ch1, 1sc in each st of Round. Ss in top of first st to connect. [120sc]

R21: Ch1, (1sc in st, sk next 2 sts, ch5) 40 times. Ss in top of first st to connect. Put Color A aside. [40sc/40 x ch5-sp]

*You will make the dc stitches in the next Round **behind** the ch5-sps. Keep the ch5-sps in front of the work.*

R22: Take Color E and attach it in any first sk st out of two between the sc stitches of the previous Round. Ch3 (first dc), make 1dc more in same sk st, 2dc in second sk st, sk next sc of Round 21, (2dc in each of the next 2 sk sts, sk next sc of Round 21) 39 times. Ss in top of first st to connect. Fasten off Color E. [160dc – which will be 40 gr of 4dc]

R23: Pick up Color A in nearest first dc of a 4dc-gr of previous Round. Ch1, (1sc in first and second dc of

INDIA WILL DAZZLE YOU WITH ITS ABUNDANT COLORS, WHICH HELP TO BRIGHTEN UP THE DARK MOMENTS

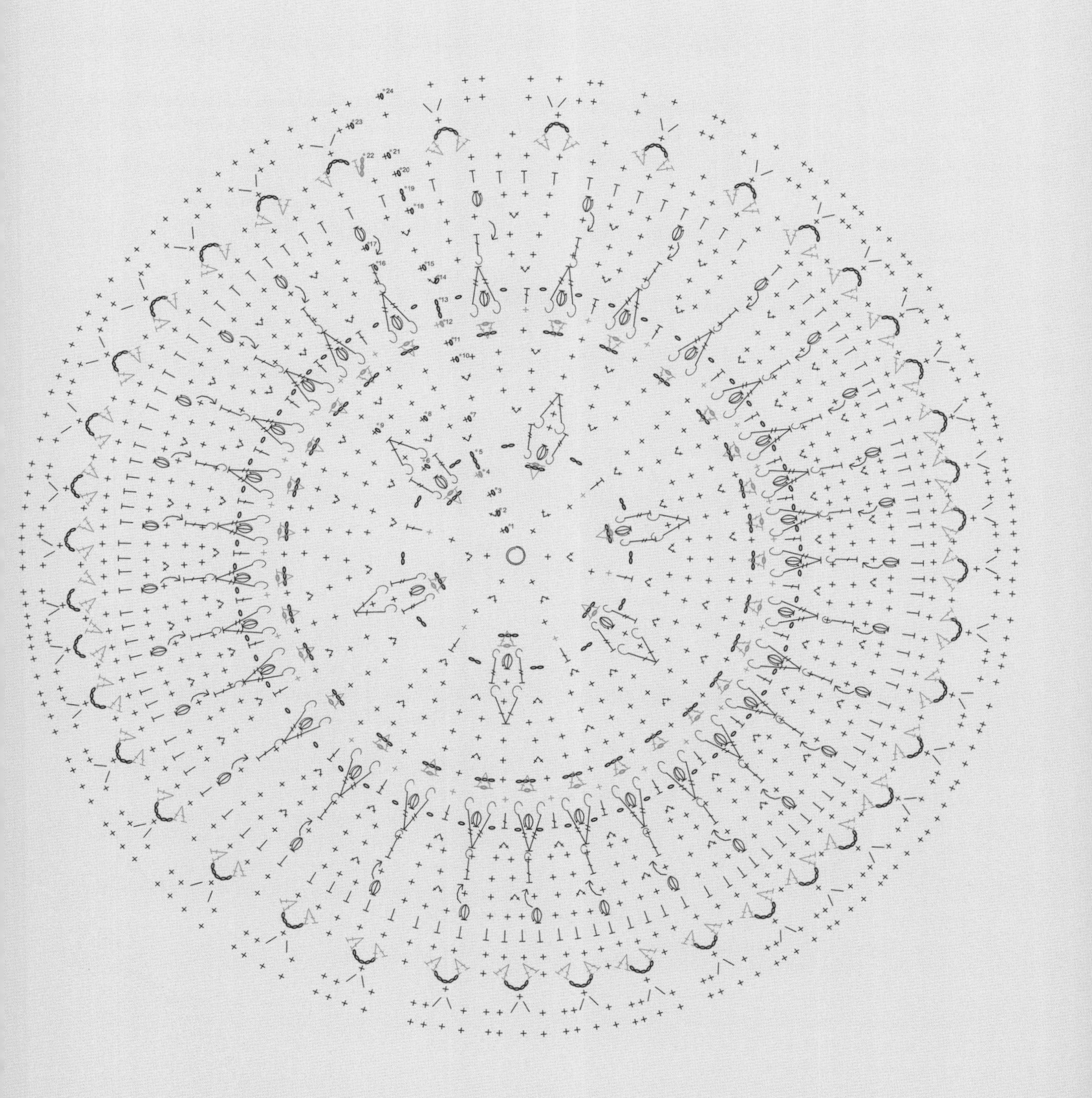

4dc-gr, 1sc through the ch5-sp of Round 21, and at the same time the third dc of the 4dc-gr, 1sc in the fourth dc of 4dc-gr] 40 times. Ss in top of first st to connect. [160sc]

R24: Ch1, 1sc in each st of Round. Ss in blo of first st to connect. [160sc]

We continue with the side of the pouf:

R25: Ch3 (first dc), 1dc in blo of each st of previous Round. Ss in top of first st to connect. Fasten off Color A. [160dc in blo]

R26: Take Color F and attach it in any st of the previous Round. Ch1, (1sc in st, sk next st, ch1) 80 times. Ss in top of first st to connect. Fasten off Color F. [80sc/80 x ch1-sp]

R27: Take Color E and attach it in any ch1-sp of the previous Round. Ch1, (1sc in ch1-sp, sk next st, ch1) 80 times. Ss in top of first st to connect. Fasten off Color E. [80sc/80 x ch1-sp]

R28: With Color D – Rep R27 [80sc/80 x ch1-sp]

R29: With Color C – Rep R27 [80sc/80 x ch1-sp]

R30: With Color B – Rep R27 [80sc/80 x ch1-sp]

R31: With Color F – Rep R27 and put Color F aside. [80sc/80 x ch1-sp]

R32: Take Color A and attach it in any ch1-sp of the previous Round. Ch3 (first dc), 1dc in next sc, (1dc in next ch1-sp, 1dc in next st) 79 times. Ss in top of first st to connect. Put Color A aside. [160dc]
R33: Pick up Color F in nearest st of previous Round. Ch1, 1sc in each st of Round. Ss in top of first st to connect. Put Color F aside. [160sc]

R34: Pick up Color A in nearest st of previous Round. Ch3 (first dc), 1dc in each st of Round. Ss in top of first st to connect. Fasten off Color A. [160dc]

R35: Pick up Color F in nearest st of previous Round – Rep R26. [80sc/80 x ch1-sp]

R36: Rep R30 [80sc/80 x ch1-sp]

R37: Rep R29 [80sc/80 x ch1-sp]

R38: Rep R28 [80sc/80 x ch1-sp]

R39: Rep R27 [80sc/80 x ch1-sp]

R40: Rep R31 – but fasten off Color F at the end of the Round. [80sc/80 x ch1-sp]

R41: Rep R32 – but fasten off Color A at the end of the Round. [160dc]

Weave in all remaining ends. For now, you have made the top of the pouf with the side. Now continue by crocheting Rounds 1-24 once more for the bottom of the pouf. Keep Color A attached in the blo of the first st just as Round 24 ends.

Stuff the top and side by putting the pouf in it.
Put the bottom part with the Right Side facing towards you on top of it. Now, make an ss through each blo of the st on the bottom and the full st on the side to connect the bottom part to the side. Once you have reached the end, fasten off Color A and weave in the remaining end.

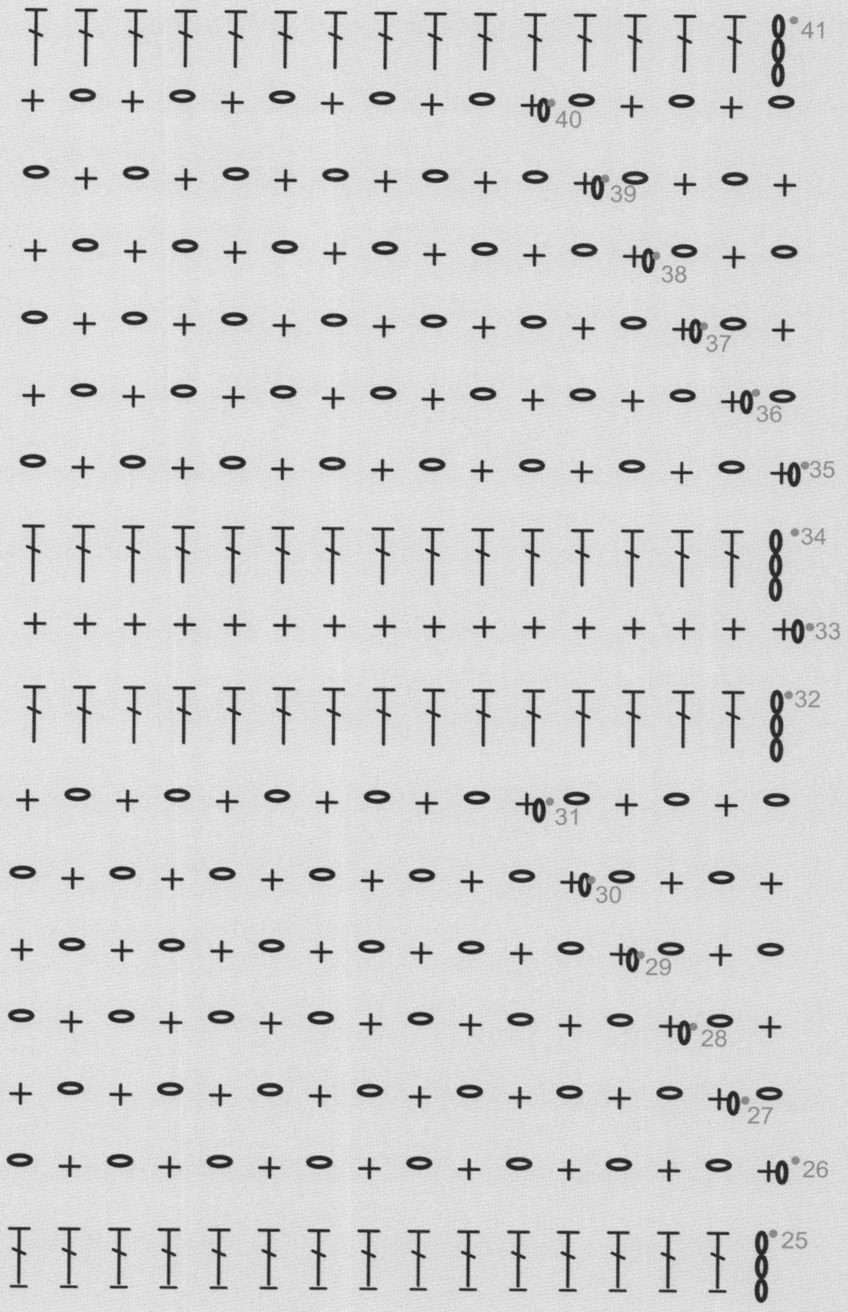

41
40
39
38
37
36
35
34
33
32
31
30
29
28
27
26
25

54°35'N, 5°55'W
• BELFAST • CLIFFS • FOLKLORE
• GIANT'S CAUSEWAY • HIKING • OCEAN

NORTHERN IRELAND

IRISH SHORES BLANKET

As a massive fan of raw, untamed nature, I decided to visit Northern Ireland a few years ago. I took a road trip along the Wild Atlantic Way, which takes you around the entire coastline of Northern Ireland. As I traveled in the Spring, I encountered all of the elements. I could be enjoying a calm breeze and some warm rays of the sun and then, an hour later, I could be in a snow flurry. I traveled through many small villages and took the opportunity to walk along rope bridges between cliffs. I visited old castles and ruins, which belonged to different clans from history. I also walked the Giant's Causeway; an incredible piece of nature that takes its name from an ancient story about a giant who used this part of the shore to walk to the other side of the ocean. The Causeway is built up from thousands of hexagonal-shaped stones. No one put them there; nature did this by itself. Each stone is carved in the same way, and they come in many sizes, ranging from the size of a mountain to small stones on which you can walk to the sea. It makes you realize nature has a soul of its own as no human hand has created such a wonder.

The Northern parts of Ireland are genuinely one of my favorite destinations of all time. Green moss, tall stones, the wild ocean, and the fog that lies over the lakes. They all combine to make Ireland a place full of ancient mystery. I love all the tales and folklore of this culture combined with the traditional Celtic beliefs and language. The Celtic marks and symbols are well known worldwide, and their cable work can be found in almost every piece of knitting and crochet in Ireland. For that reason, I tried to create a pattern that represents all those things. The Celtic cable symbolizes the wild ocean's rushing water, combined with the colors you find in the nature of Ireland.

PATTERN

With Color A and crochet hook size 5.0mm (H/8), ch18.

R1 (WS): Make a sc in the second ch from the hook. Make a sc in each ch. Turn. [17sc]

R2 (RS): Ch1 (does not count as st here and throughout entire pattern), 1sc in next 2 sts, 1sc in blo of next 13 sts, 1sc in next 2 sts. Turn. [4sc/13sc in blo]

R3 and all odd Rows (WS): Ch2 (does not count as st here and throughout entire pattern), 1hdc in each st on Row. Turn. [17hdc]

R4 (RS): Ch1, 1sc in next 3 sts, 1tr in the third flo of Row 2 (*this will be the 5th actual st in Row 2*), sk st, 1sc in next st, 1tr in the same flo you just used, sk st, 1sc in next st, 1tr in the seventh flo of Row 2 (*this will be the 9th actual st in Row 2*), sk st, 1sc in next st, 1tr in the same flo you just used, sk st, 1sc in next st, 1tr in the eleventh flo of Row 2 (*this will be the 13th actual st in Row 2*), sk st, 1sc in next st, 1tr in the same flo you just used, sk st, 1sc in next 3 sts. Turn. [11sc/6tr]

R6 (RS): Ch1, 1sc in next 2 sts, 1fptr around the first tr of Row 4, sk st, (1sc in next 3 sts, 1fptr2tog over next 2 tr stitches of Row 4, sk st) twice, 1sc in next 3 sts, 1fptr around the last tr of Row 4, sk st, 1sc in next 2 sts. Turn. [13sc/2fptr/2fptr2tog]

R8 (RS): Ch1, 1sc in next 3 sts, 1fptr around the first fptr of Row 6, sk st, (1sc in next st, 1fptr around next fptr2tog of Row 6, sk st, 1sc in next st, 1fptr around the same fptr2tog you just used, sk st) twice, 1sc in next st, 1fptr around the last fptr of Row 6, sk st, 1sc in next 3 sts. Turn. [11sc/6fptr]

R10 (RS): Ch1, 1sc in next 4 sts, (1fptr2tog over next 2 fptr of Row 8, sk st, 1sc in next 3 sts) twice, 1fptr2tog over next 2 fptr of Row 8, sk st, 1sc in next 4 sts. Turn. [14sc/3 x fptr2tog]

R12 (RS): Ch1, 1sc in next 3 sts, (1fptr around next fptr2tog of Row 10, sk st, 1sc in next st, 1fptr around same fptr2tog you just used, sk st, 1sc in next st) 3 times. 1sc in next 2 sts. Turn. [11sc/6fptr]

R14 (RS): Ch1, 1sc in next 2 sts, 1fptr around first fptr two Rows down, sk st, (1sc in next 3 sts, 1fptr2tog over next 2 fptr stitches two Rows down, sk st) twice, 1sc in next 3 sts, 1fptr around last fptr two Rows down, sk st, 1sc in next 2 sts. Turn. [13sc/2fptr/2 x fptr2tog]

HOOK SIZE NEEDED: 5.0MM (H/8) HOOK

YARN NEEDED: SCHEEPJES SKIES HEAVY COMES IN HANKS OF 100G (3½OZ) WITH A LENGTH OF 170M (185YDS) OF YARN. THE YARN CONSISTS OF 100% PREMIUM BLEND COTTON.

- 2 HANKS OF SCHEEPJES SKIES HEAVY 108 CIRCUMCUMULUS (COLOR A)
- 2 HANKS OF SCHEEPJES SKIES HEAVY 105 STRATUS (COLOR B)
- 2 HANKS OF SCHEEPJES SKIES HEAVY 103 ALTOCUMULUS (COLOR C)
- 2 HANKS OF SCHEEPJES SKIES HEAVY 100 CIRROCUMULUS (COLOR D)
- 2 HANKS OF SCHEEPJES SKIES HEAVY 102 CUMULUS (COLOR E)
- 2 HANKS OF SCHEEPJES SKIES HEAVY 104 ALTOSTRATUS (COLOR F)
- 2 HANKS OF SCHEEPJES SKIES HEAVY 107 CUMULONIMBUS (COLOR G)
- 1 HANK OF SCHEEPJES SKIES HEAVY 106 CIRROSTRATUS (COLOR H)

R16 (RS): Ch1, 1sc in next 3 sts, 1fptr around first fptr two Rows down, sk st, (1sc in next st, 1fptr around next fptr2tog two Rows down, sk st, 1sc in next st, 1fptr around the same fptr2tog you just used, sk st) twice, 1sc in next st, 1fptr around the last fptr two Rows down, sk st, 1sc in next 3 sts. Turn. [11sc/6fptr]

R18 (RS): Ch1, 1sc in next 4 sts, (1fptr2tog over next 2 fptr two Rows down, sk st, 1sc in next 3 sts) 3 times, 1sc in last st. Turn. [14sc/3 x fptr2tog]

R20 (RS): Ch1, 1sc in next 3 sts, (1fptr around next fptr2tog two Rows down, sk st, 1sc in next st, 1fptr around same fptr2tog you just used, sk st, 1sc in next st) 3 times. 1sc in next 2 sts. Turn. [11sc/6fptr]

R21 (WS): Rep Row 3. [17hdc]

Now Repeat **Rows 14-21** another 16 times.
After you have done this, repeat **Rows 14-19** one more time. Turn work and make a sc in each stitch on Row. Keep the yarn attached.

OTHER MATERIALS NEEDED:
STITCH MARKERS

SIZE OF PROJECT: THE BLANKET WILL HAVE A WIDTH OF 101CM (40IN) AND A LENGTH OF 140CM (55IN).

TIPS FOR THIS PATTERN:

- THE BLANKET IS MADE UP OF LONG, INDIVIDUAL STRIPES. IN THIS WAY, YOU WILL CROCHET SMALL PARTS THAT YOU WILL JOIN TO FORM THE BLANKET.
- ON EACH ODD ROW EXCEPT THE FIRST ONE, YOU WILL CROCHET HDC ROWS. AT THE TURN AND START OF THOSE ROWS, YOU WILL MAKE A CH2. THIS CH2 DOES NOT COUNT AS A STITCH; THIS MEANS YOU WILL MAKE A REGULAR HDC IN THE FIRST STITCH. YOU WILL MAKE THE CH2 TO OBTAIN HEIGHT AND AVOID ANY GAPS ON THE SIDE.
- WHEN MAKING THE LAST STITCH ON EVEN ROWS, YOU MUST COMPLETE THE LAST STITCH IN THE CH2 THAT DOES NOT COUNT AS A STITCH. IT MEANS YOU SKIP THE ACTUAL LAST HDC AND MAKE THE STITCH IN THE CH. BY DOING THIS, THE SIDE OF THE STRIPE WILL BE STRAIGHTER.
- IN THE PATTERN, YOU WILL MAKE FRONT POST STITCHES. WHEN MAKING A FRONT POST STITCH, YOU ALWAYS SKIP A STITCH BEHIND IT.
- THE PATTERN IS WORKED IN ROWS. ALL THE EVEN ROWS WILL BE ON THE RIGHT SIDE OF THE WORK, ALL ODD ROWS WILL BE ON THE WRONG SIDE OF THE WORK.
- THE COLORED SECTION OF THIS PATTERN'S CHART INDICATES THE REPEATING ROWS.

Now you are going to crochet sc stitches all around the stripe you just made. It will be the most straight-forward way to join the stripes later without any trouble. So, let us continue to the point where your yarn is still attached.

Ch1 and turn to the long side of the stripe. Start making sc stitches in the side. The total amount of sc stitches you make along the long side is not essential, as long as you divide them equally and make the same amount of stitches on the other long side and all other long sides of the other stripes. I made one sc in each Row end. When you reach the end of the long side, make an sc-ch2-sc in the first st of the short side. Make 1sc in the next 15 sts, make 1sc-ch2-1sc in the last st of the short side. Turn to the long opposite side and crochet the same amount of sts you made on the other long side. After it, you will reach the second short side. Make an sc-ch2-sc in the first st of the second short side, make 1sc in the next 15 sts, make 1sc-ch2-1sc in the last st of the second short side, and make an ss in the first st on the long side to connect. Fasten off yarn and weave in all remaining ends.

Make six more stripes with **Color B–G.**

Connecting the Stripes:
Once you finished all seven stripes, it is time to join them. You will connect them in the order of the colors. So Color A must be connected with Color B, Color B must be connected to Color C, etc.

To combine two stripes, lay them together at the long side with the Wrong Side facing each other. You can use stitch markers to hold them together. It means on both stripes, the Right Side will be visible while joining. Take Color H and attach it through both ch2-crns of both stripes on the Right Side of the work and make a sc in it. Now create an sc through each st of both stripes to connect them. If you made the same amount of stitches on all long sides, the number of stitches should match. Once you reach the ch2-crns at the other end of the stripes, make sc through both ch2-crns and fasten off Color H. Weave in both ends. Repeat this procedure until all seven stripes are connected.

The Border:
Now attach Color H in a ch2-crn that is on one of the blanket's four corners. You will start crocheting on the short side of the blanket. Ch2 (doesn't count as st), *1hdc-ch2-1hdc in ch2-crn, 1hdc in next 19 sts, (1hdc in next ch2-crn, 1ss in sc of joining seam, 1hdc in next ch2-crn of next stripe, 1hdc in next 19 sts) 6 times. 1hdc-ch2-1hdc in next ch2-crn, turn to the long side and make a hdc in each st on the long side. Repeat from * one more time. Ss in first st made to connect. Fasten off Color H. Weave in ends.

Optional: You can add some tassels to your blanket. I added one tassel of each Color used at the short sides of the blanket. I attached one on the two corners and at each ss, made in a joining seam.

Make a tassel by cutting 5 or 6 threads approx. 30cm (12in). Wrap these threads around your fingers. Now lay the wrapping thread on the point where you want to attach the tassel. Pull the thread with your crochet hook partly through the stitch. Once the string is through the stitch, divide the other threads equally on both sides. Now make a slipknot by using both sides of the thread and pull it up tight. Once you have completed all 8 tassels on a side, cut them all the same length. If you find making tassels tricky, check out my website for a full explanation of this process.

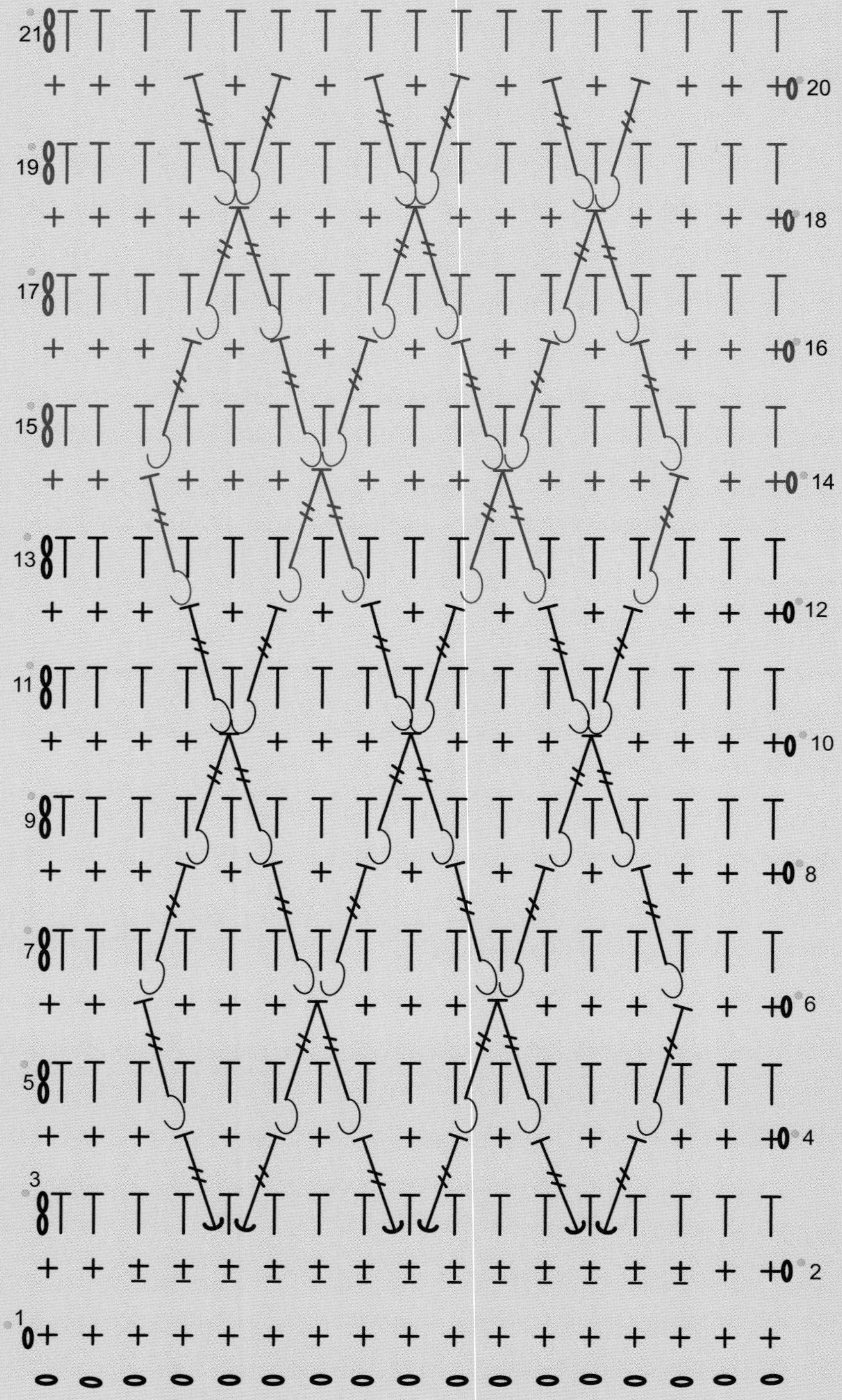

21
20
19
18
17
16
15
14
13
12
11
10
9
8
7
6
5
4
3
2
1

I DECIDED TO
TAKE A ROAD TRIP
ALONG THE WILD
ATLANTIC WAY

38° 42' NB, 9° 8' WL
• CAPITAL • TILES • MOSAIC
• FADO • ROSSIO • TRAM LINE

PORTUGAL (LISBON)

PORTUGUESE TILES

Anyone who has been to Portugal will have seen the famous tiles found on almost every single wall as you walk along the streets. They come in virtually every color, format, and design possible. There is even a museum in Lisbon containing hundreds of tile patterns and examples. The tiles are the first thing that came to mind when I think about my visit to Lisbon a few years ago, and another memory is attached to them.

When I was planning my trip to Lisbon, I researched places in the city that are still relatively unknown, and I found a great story about a tourist who was told by a local to visit the cemetery. Yes, the cemetery! And as locals know the best places to visit, I decided to see it while I was in Lisbon. I took the metro line, along an old track through the city in a classic, yellow metro vehicle. Just that is an experience in itself! Once I reached the stop at the cemetery, I got off and entered through a large gate. I started walking and didn't know where to look at first as there was so much to see.

It was like I had entered a small mini-village surrounded by silence and nature. I saw that every grave holds a small house in which the coffin stands. And those houses come in all sorts of shapes, styles, and decoration. Some have been reclaimed by nature and are now surrounded by grass and tree roots; others are well taken care of and have the most beautiful, shiny tiled walls. Each house makes you wonder who owns it and how it may look from the inside.

I spent a whole afternoon in absolute wonder at the vivid details of this cemetery, which is called "Prazeres." It was far more exciting and much richer with tiles than the tourist places in the city and it was the inspiration for me to start creating mosaic tile patterns. I have made different designs and patterns in the past, and created a new one for this book, so here are the Portuguese Tiles. I have used them to make a pretty throw pillow, but they could also be used to create a throw.

PATTERN

With Color A and crochet hook size 3.0mm (C2/D3), make a ML.

R1 (RS): ch2 (first hdc), make 11hdc more in the loop. Ss in top of first st to connect. Put Color A aside. [12hdc]

R2: Take Color B and attach in blo of any st. Ch1 (doesn't count as st here and throughout entire pattern), (2sc in blo, ch2, 1sc in blo) 4 times. Ss in top of first st to connect. Put Color B aside. [4 sides of 3sc and 4 x ch2-crn]

R3: Pick up Color A in blo of second st on the nearest side. Ch1, *1dc in flo, 1sc in blo, 1sc in the first ch of ch2-crn, ch2, 1sc in the second ch from ch2-crn, 1sc in blo. Rep from * 3 more times. Ss in top of first st to connect. Put Color A aside. [4 sides of 4sc/1dc and 4 x ch2-crn]

R4: Pick up Color B in blo of third st on the nearest side, which will be a dc. Ch1, *1sc in blo, 1dc in flo, 1sc in blo, 1sc in the first ch of ch2-crn, ch2, 1sc in the second ch from ch2-crn, 1sc in blo, 1dc in flo. Rep from * 3 more times. Ss in top of first st to connect. Put Color B aside. [4 sides of 5sc/2dc and 4 x ch2-crn]

R5: Pick up Color A in blo of fourth st on the nearest side, which will be an sc between two dc stitches. Ch1, *1dc in flo, 3sc in blo, 1sc in the first ch of ch2-crn, ch2, 1sc in the second ch from ch2-crn, 3sc in blo. Rep from * 3 more times. Ss in top of first st to connect. Put Color A aside. [4 sides of 8sc/1dc and 4 x ch2-crn]

R6: Pick up Color B in blo of fifth st on the nearest side, which will be a dc. Ch1, *2sc in blo, 1dc in flo, 2sc in blo, 1sc in the first ch of ch2-crn, ch2, 1sc in the second ch from ch2-crn, 2sc in blo, 1dc in flo, 1sc in blo. Rep from * 3 more times. Ss in top of first st to connect. Fasten off Color B. [4 sides of 9sc/2dc and 4 x ch2-crn]

R7: Pick up Color A in blo of sixth st on the nearest side. Ch1, *1sc in blo, 1dc in flo, 4sc in blo, 1sc in the first ch of ch2-crn, ch2, 1sc in the second ch from ch2-crn, 4sc in blo, 1dc in flo. Rep from * 3 more times. Ss in top of first st to connect. Put Color A aside. [4 sides of 11sc/2dc and 4 x ch2-crn]

R8: Take Color C and attach it in blo of seventh st on any side. Ch1, *1dc in flo, 2sc in blo, 1dc in flo, 3sc in blo, 1sc in the first ch of ch2-crn, ch2, 1sc in the second

HOOK SIZE NEEDED: 3.0MM (C2/D3) HOOK

YARN NEEDED: SCHEEPJES CATONA COMES IN BALLS OF 50G (1¾OZ) WITH A LENGTH OF 125M (136YDS) OF YARN. THE YARN CONSISTS OF 100% MERCERIZED COTTON.

- 4 BALLS OF SCHEEPJES CATONA 527 MIDNIGHT (COLOR A)
- 1 BALL OF SCHEEPJES CATONA 106 SNOW WHITE (COLOR B)
- 1 BALL OF SCHEEPJES CATONA 105 BRIDAL WHITE (COLOR C)
- 1 BALL OF SCHEEPJES CATONA 505 LINEN (COLOR D)
- 1 BALL OF SCHEEPJES CATONA 404 ENGLISH TEA (COLOR E)

OTHER MATERIALS NEEDED: A CUSHION INNER OF SIZE 40 X 40CM (16 X 16IN)

SIZE OF PROJECT: A SINGLE TILE WILL HAVE A LENGTH AND HEIGHT OF APPROX. 18 X 18CM (7 X 7IN). THE FINISHED CUSHION WILL BE AROUND 40 X 40CM (16 X 16IN).

ch from ch2-crn, 3sc in blo, 1dc in flo, 2sc in blo. Rep from * 3 more times. Ss in top of first st to connect. Put Color C aside. [4 sides of 12sc/3dc and 4 x ch2-crn]

R9: Pick up Color A in blo of eighth st on the nearest side. Ch1, *2sc in blo, 1dc in flo, 3sc in blo, 1dc in flo, 1sc in blo, 1sc in the first ch of ch2-crn, ch2, 1sc in the second ch from ch2-crn, 1sc in blo, 1dc in flo, 3sc in blo, 1dc in flo, 1sc in blo. Rep from * 3 more times. Ss in top of first st to connect.
Put Color A aside. [4 sides of 13sc/4dc and 4 x ch2-crn]

R10: Pick up Color C in blo of ninth st on the nearest side. Ch1, *(1sc in blo, 1dc in flo) twice, 5sc in blo, 1sc in the first ch of ch2-crn, ch2, 1sc in the second ch from ch2-crn, 5sc in blo, 1dc in flo, 1sc in blo, 1dc in flo. Rep from * 3 more times. Ss in top of first st to connect. Fasten off Color C. [4 sides of 15sc/4dc and 4 x ch2-crn]

R11: Pick up Color A in blo of tenth st on the nearest side. Ch1, *(2sc in blo, 1dc in flo) twice, 1sc in blo, 1dc in flo, 2sc in blo, 1sc in the first ch of ch2-crn, ch2, 1sc in the second ch from ch2-crn, 2sc in blo, 1dc in flo, 1sc in

TIPS FOR THIS PATTERN:

- THIS PATTERN IS MADE USING THE MOSAIC TECHNIQUE. FOR THIS PATTERN, WE WORK ALL SC STITCHES IN THE BACK LOOP OF THE STS - EXCEPT THE CORNER STS WHICH YOU MAKE IN THE CHS.
- IN THE PATTERN, YOU MAKE DC STITCHES IN THE FRONT LOOP OF THE STITCH TWO ROUNDS DOWN. IF YOU MAKE A DC IN R4, YOU WILL USE THE FLO OF THE ST UNDER IT IN R2. YOU ALWAYS SKIP A ST ON THE CURRENT ROUND WHEN MAKING A DC. I HAVE NOT WRITTEN THIS IN THE DIRECTIONS, SO KEEP THIS IN MIND.
- THE PATTERN IS WORKED IN THE ROUND. IT MEANS YOU WORK ON THE RIGHT SIDE AT ALL TIMES.
- WHEN PICKING UP A COLOR, YOU ALWAYS DO THAT IN THE BACK LOOP OF THE INDICATED ST.
- WHEN CONNECTING A ROUND WITH AN SS,YOU WILL MAKE AN SS THROUGH THE FULL ST.
- WHEN THE PATTERN TELLS YOU TO MAKE 2SC IN BLO, YOU CROCHET 1SC IN BLO OF THE NEXT TWO STS. THE SAME GOES FOR DC STITCHES. IF THE PATTERN TELLS YOU TO MAKE A DC IN FLO, YOU WILL CROCHET 1DC IN THE FLO OF THE ST UNDER IT TWO ROWS DOWN.
- THE FIRST ST ON A ROUND IS ALSO MADE IN THE JOINING ST. WHEN YOU HAVE TO START WITH A DC IN THE FIRST ST, YOU WILL MAKE THAT DC ON THE POINT OF JOINING TWO ROUNDS DOWN.
- THE TILE PATTERN IS USED TO CREATE A CUSHION COVER; HOWEVER, IT CAN ALSO CREATE A THROW OR OTHER PROJECTS.
- THE DIAGRAM SHOWS ONLY ONE SIDE OF THE PATTERN. YOU CAN EASILY READ THIS BY STARTING IN THE MIDDLE POINT, WORKING THE RIGHT SIDE AFTER THE MIDDLE POINT, AND THEN WORKING THE LEFT SIDE OF THE SAME ROW.

* 3 more times. Ss in top of first st to connect. Put Color A aside. [4 sides of 15sc/6dc and 4 x ch2-crn]

R12: Take Color D and attach it in blo of eleventh st on any side. Ch1, *1dc in flo, 2sc in blo, 1dc in flo, 7sc in blo, 1sc in the first ch of ch2-crn, ch2, 1sc in the second ch from ch2-crn, 7sc in blo, 1dc in flo, 2sc in blo. Rep from * 3 more times. Ss in top of first st to connect. Put Color D aside. [4 sides of 20sc/3dc and 4 x ch2-crn]

R13: Pick up Color A in blo of twelfth st on the nearest side. Ch1, *1sc in blo, 1dc in flo, 4sc in blo, 1dc in flo, 5sc in blo, 1sc in the first ch of ch2-crn, ch2, 1sc in the second ch from ch2-crn, 5sc in blo, 1dc in flo, 4sc in blo, 1dc in flo. Rep from * 3 more times. Ss in top of first st to connect. Put Color A aside. [4 sides of 21sc/4dc and 4 x ch2-crn]

R14: Pick up Color D in blo of thirteenth st on the nearest side. Ch1, *2sc in blo, 1dc in flo, 7sc in blo, 1dc in flo, 2sc in blo, 1sc in the first ch of ch2-crn, ch2, 1sc in the second ch from ch2-crn, 2sc in blo, 1dc in flo, 7sc in blo, 1dc in flo, 1sc in blo. Rep from * 3 more times. Ss in top of first st to connect. Fasten off Color D. [4 sides of 23sc/4dc and 4 x ch2-crn]

R15: Pick up Color A in blo of fourteenth st on the nearest side. Ch1, *(1dc in flo, 3sc in blo) 3 times, 2sc in blo, 1sc in the first ch of ch2-crn, ch2, 1sc in the second ch from ch2-crn, 2sc in blo, (3sc in blo, 1dc in flo) twice, 3sc in blo. Rep from * 3 more times. Ss in top of first st to connect. Put Color A aside. [4 sides of 24sc/5dc and 4 x ch2-crn]

R16: Take Color E and attach it in blo of fifteenth st of any side. Ch1, *(1sc in blo, 1dc in flo) 2 times, 5sc in blo, 1dc in flo, 5sc in blo, 1sc in the first ch of ch2-crn, ch2, 1sc in the second ch from ch2-crn, 5sc in blo, 1dc in flo, 5sc in blo, 1dc in flo, 1sc in blo, 1dc in flo. Rep from * 3 more times. Ss in top of first st to connect. Put Color E aside. [4 sides of 25sc/6dc and 4 x ch2-crn]

R17: Pick up Color A in blo of sixteenth st on the nearest side. Ch1, *1dc in flo, 4sc in blo, 1dc in flo, 1sc in blo, 1dc in flo, 2sc in blo, 1dc in flo, 5sc in blo, 1sc in the first ch of ch2-crn, ch2, 1sc in the second ch from ch2-crn, 5sc in blo, 1dc in flo, 2sc in blo, 1dc in flo, 1sc in blo, 1dc in flo, 4sc in blo. Rep from * 3 more times. Ss in top of first st to connect. Put Color A aside. [4 sides of 26sc/7dc and 4 x ch2-crn]

R18: Pick up Color E in blo of seventeenth st on the nearest side. Ch1, *2sc in blo, 1dc in flo, 1sc in blo, 1dc in flo, 3sc in blo, 1dc in flo, 8sc in blo, 1sc in the first ch of ch2-crn, ch2, 1sc in the second ch from ch2-crn, 8sc in blo, 1dc in flo, 3sc in blo, (1dc in flo, 1sc in blo) twice. Rep from * 3 more times. Ss in top of first st to connect. Fasten off Color E. [4 sides of 29sc/6dc and 4 x ch2-crn]

R19: Pick up Color A in blo of eighteenth st on the nearest side. Ch1, *1sc in blo, 1dc in flo, 4sc in blo, 1dc in flo, 2sc in blo, 1dc in flo, 8sc in blo, 1sc in the first ch of ch2-crn, ch2, 1sc in the second ch from ch2-crn, 8sc in blo, 1dc in flo, 2sc in blo, 1dc in flo, 4sc in blo, 1dc in flo. Rep from * 3 more times. Ss in top of first st to connect. Fasten off Color A. [4 sides of 31sc/6dc and 4 x ch2-crn]

Weave in all ends and block the tile.
You have now finished one tile. Make seven more for a total of eight pieces. For each side of the cover, we will

THE TILES ARE THE FIRST THING THAT CAME TO MIND WHEN I THINK ABOUT MY VISIT TO LISBON

use four tiles that you need to join. Make sure the tiles line up perfectly so that the lines will continue between the tiles.

To connect the tiles for one side, lay two tiles together with the Right Side facing each other. So, you will work on the Wrong Side. Take Color A and attach it through both ch2-crns of both tiles. Now make a sc in the ch2-crn and an ss through both stitches of the tiles all along to the next ch2-crn, make an sc through the ch2-crns. Fasten off Color A. Now you have connected two tiles. Repeat this with the following two tiles.

You now will have 2 tiles connected twice. Connect those two pieces in the same way as you did between the separate tiles. So, you make a sc in all ch2-crns and an ss in the regular sts. Once this is done, you will have 4 tiles connected.

Take Color A and attach it in any ch2-crn of one of the four crns of the cover. Ch3 (doesn't count as st), *3dc in ch2-crn, 1dc in each st to next ch2-crn, 1dc in next ch2-crn, sk the connection seam, 1dc in next ch2-crn of next tile, 1dc in each st to next ch2-crn. Rep from * 3 more times. Ss in top of first st to connect. Fasten off Color A. Weave in all remaining ends.

Repeat the same process with the other four tiles to create a second side for the cover. You will now have two sides of four tiles with a dc border around them. Lay those sides together, so they have the Wrong Side facing. It means you will be working on the Right Side of the work. Take Color A and start crocheting sc stitches through each st of both sides to connect them. Make sure to do this equally on both sides. Once you've closed three sides, insert the cushion inner and close the fourth side as well by making sc stitches through sts on both sides—Ss in top of first st to connect. Fasten off Color A and weave in the remaining ends.

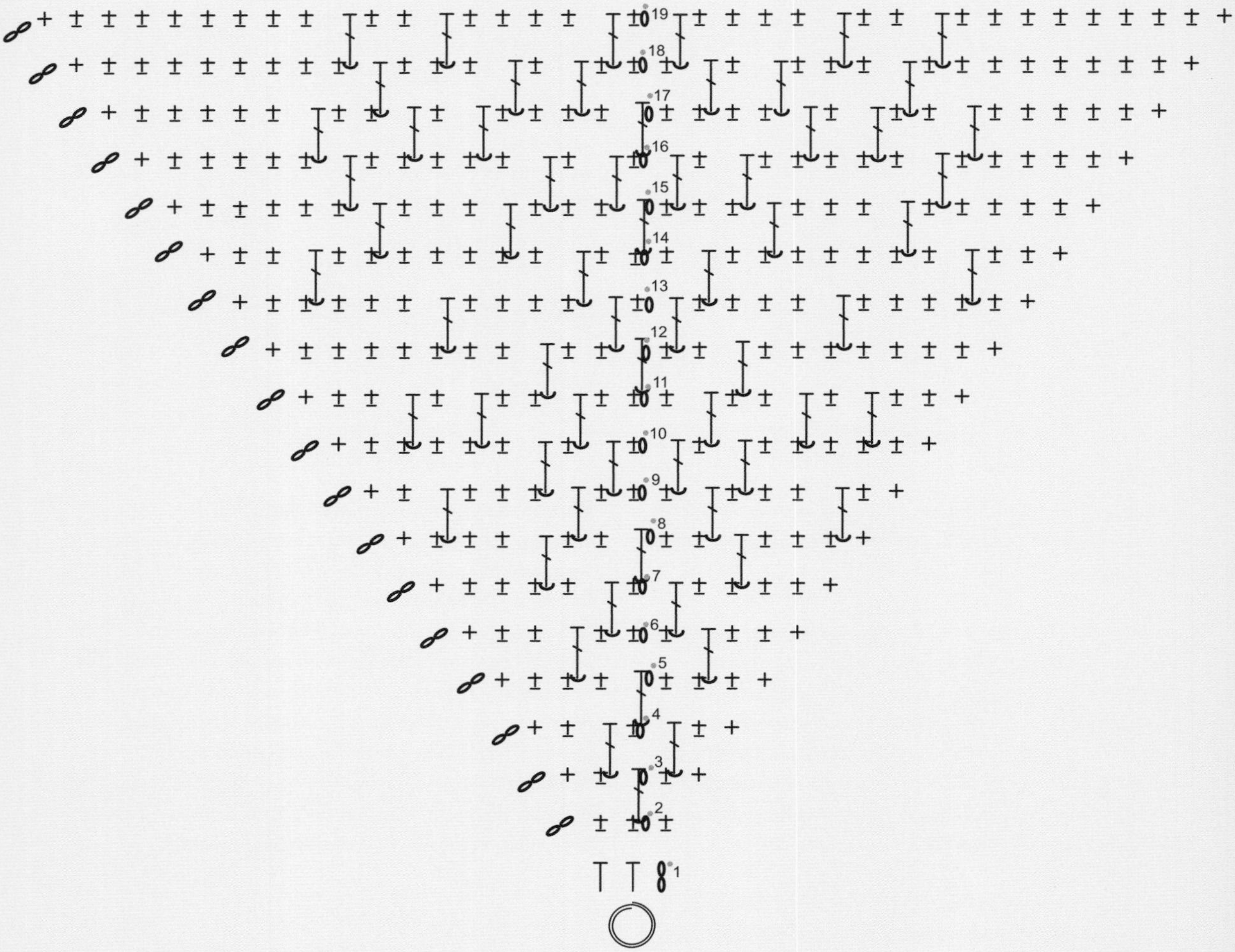

19
18
17
16
15
14
13
12
11
10
9
8
7
6
5
4
3
2
1

I TOOK THE OLD
METRO LINE, WHICH
WAS SUCH A
GREAT EXPERIENCE

8° 39' S, 115° 13' E
• ISLAND • LOTUS FLOWERS • CARVINGS
• BEACH • COCKTAILS • TEMPLE

INDONESIA (BALI)

KETUT'S MANDALA

I decided to start my journey to Indonesia in Sumatra, from where I traveled right across Java. My end destination was Bali, the island which lies near Java. Bali is the most "touristy" place of the islands, containing many resorts and beaches. Before I reached the coastline – where the luxurious life of swimming, sun, and cocktails could begin, I decided to investigate Bali by visiting the larger cities.

Halfway through the journey, I settled down in Ubud, a small town full of artisan crafts and artists. At breakfast, I heard someone behind me talking about visiting the fortune teller Ketut. Many of you who have seen the movie *Eat, Pray, Love* might recognize this name. Although the real Ketut isn't in the film, he does exist! I asked a taxi driver to take me to where he lived in a small village some miles away from Ubud. Once I entered, I realized I wasn't the only one who would visit him that day. I walked in and paid the price for a consultation with Ketut, and I got a paper number. It showed the number "14", which meant I was 14th in line, but it was strange as 14 is also the day of my birth!

I walked along the garden, with impressive wooden birdcages, a pond full of lotus flowers, and the most exotic flora. Finally, it was my turn to meet Ketut, who was sitting on his porch. The man only had two teeth left and looked very ancient. He asked for my hand and started telling me things about me that he couldn't know and about something that would happen in the future. It was a special moment, and although it was more than ten years ago, I can still hear his words today. Although I only spoke to the man for about twenty minutes, I still believe his words left a mark on my soul. For that reason, I decided to dedicate this pattern to him. Inspired by the purple lotus flowers on his pond and the carved figures in his porch, this pattern is my memory of Ketut's place.

HE ASKED FOR MY
HAND AND STARTED
TELLING ME THINGS

PATTERN

With crochet hook size 3.0mm (C2/D3) and the yarn, make a ML.

R1 (RS): Ch3 (first dc), make 11dc more in the loop. Ss in top of first st to connect. [12dc]

R2: Ch1 (doesn't count as st here and throughout entire pattern), 2sc in each st of Round. Ss in flo of first st made to connect. [24sc]

The next Round can ruffle or get your work out of shape; this is normal.

R3: *starting in flo of first st of previous Round.* Ch4 (first tr), 1tr in flo of each st of Round. Ss in top of first st to connect. [24tr in flo]

R4: Ch1, 1sc through tr and at the same time the blo behind the tr which you left unworked – as you only used the flo in Round 3. Rep this process with every st on Round. The tr stitches will bend backward. Ss in top of first st to connect. [24sc]

R5: Ch3 (first dc), 1dc in same st, 1dc in next st, (2dc in next st, 1dc in next st) 11 times. Ss in top of first st to connect. [36dc]

R6: Ch1, (1sc in next st, ch5, sk next 2 sts) 12 times. Ss in top of first st to connect. Ss to middle ch of next ch5-sp. [12sc/12 x ch5-sp]

R7: Ch1, (1sc in next ch5-sp, ch7) 12 times. Ss in top of first st to connect. Ss to middle ch of next ch7-sp. [12sc/12 x ch7-sp]

R8: Ch1, (1sc in next ch7-sp, ch7) 12 times. Ss in top of first st to connect. 1ss to next ch7-sp. [12sc/12 x ch7-sp]

R9: *Starting in ch7-sp.* Ch3 (first dc), 6dc in the same ch7-sp, sk next st, (7dc in next ch7-sp, sk next st) 11 times. Ss in top of first st to connect. [12 gr of 7dc]

R10: Ch2 (this will be the first dc of a dc2tog), 1dc in next st (this will be the second dc of a dc2tog), 1dc in next 3 sts, 1dc2tog over next 2 sts, ch3, *1dc2tog over next 2 sts, 1dc in next 3 sts, 1dc2tog over next 2 sts, ch3. Rep from * 10 more times. Ss in top of first st made – which will be the first regular dc and not the ch2 of the dc2tog. [12 gr of dc2tog-3dc-dc2tog and 12 x ch3-sp]

R11: Ch2 (this will be the first dc of a dc2tog), 1dc in next st (this will be the second dc of a dc2tog), 1dc in

<u>HOOK SIZE NEEDED:</u> 3.0MM (C2/D3) HOOK

<u>YARN NEEDED:</u> 3 BALLS OF SCHEEPJES COTTON 8 COLORWAY 656 (BEIGE), WHICH COMES IN BALLS OF 50G (1¾OZ) WITH A LENGTH OF 170M (185YDS) OF YARN. THE YARN CONSISTS OF 100% COTTON.

<u>OTHER MATERIALS NEEDED:</u>
OPTIONAL IS A METAL RING WITH A DIAMETER OF 56CM (22IN) TO FRAME THE MANDALA.

<u>SIZE OF PROJECT:</u> THE MANDALA'S DIAMETER WILL BE APPROXIMATELY 56CM (22IN) AFTER BLOCKING OR CROCHETING IT INTO A RING.

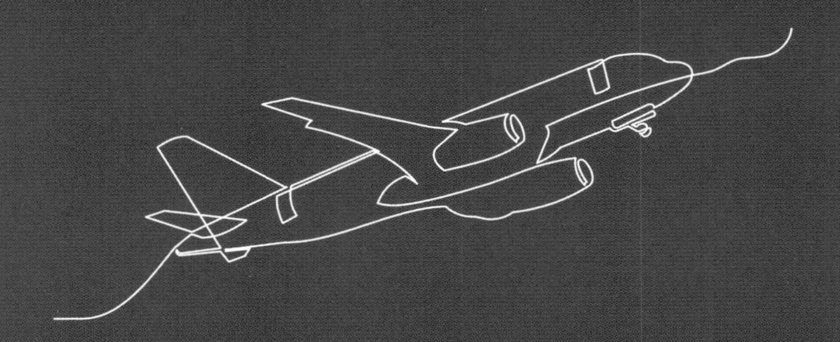

next st, 1dc2tog over next 2 sts, ch3, 1pc in next ch3-sp, ch3. *1dc2tog over next 2 sts, 1dc in next st, 1dc2tog over next 2 sts, ch3, 1pc in next ch3-sp, ch3. Rep from * 10 more times. Ss in top of first st made – which will be the first regular dc and not the ch2 of the dc2tog. [12 gr of dc2tog-1dc-dc2tog /12 pc and 24 x ch3-sp]

TIPS FOR THIS PATTERN:

- THE PATTERN IS WORKED IN THE ROUNDS, SO YOU WILL WORK THE RIGHT SIDE OF THE DESIGN AT ALL TIMES.
- THE PATTERN CAN RUFFLE OR BOBBLE A BIT WHILE CROCHETING IT. FOR THIS REASON, IT MUST BE BLOCKED FOR A PERFECT OUTCOME – OR CROCHETED INTO A RING.
- THE STITCH YOU START A ROUND WITH WILL ALWAYS BE MADE IN THE JOINING STITCH.
- THE DIAGRAM FOR THIS PATTERN CONTAINS THE COMPLETE CENTER OF THE MANDALA. THE BORDER IS SHOWN AS A SMALL CUT-OUT AS THESE ARE JUST REPEATS OVER THE ENTIRE ROUND.

R12: Ch2 (this will be the first dc of a dc3tog), finish the dc3tog over the next 2 sts, ch4, 1pc in next ch3-sp, ch4, sk next pc, 1pc in next ch3-sp, ch4. *1dc3tog over next 3 sts, ch4, 1pc in next ch3-sp, ch4, sk next pc, 1pc in next ch3-sp, ch4. Rep from * 10 more times. Ss in top of first st – which will be the finished dc3tog and not the ch2 you started with. [12 x dc3tog /24pc/36 x ch4-sp]

R13: Ch6 (first dc + ch3), (1pc in next ch4-sp, ch3, sk next pc) twice, 1pc in next ch4-sp, ch3. *1dc in next st, ch3, (1pc in next ch4-sp, ch3, sk next pc) twice, 1pc in next ch4-sp, ch3. Rep from * 10 more times. Ss in third ch to connect. [12dc/36pc/48 x ch3-sp]

R14: Ch1, *1sc in dc, 1sc in next ch3-sp, ch7, sk next pc, 1sc in next ch3-sp, 1sc in next pc, 1sc in next ch3-sp, ch7, sk next pc, 1sc in next ch3-sp. Rep from * 11 more times. Ss in top of first st to connect. Ss to next ch7-sp. [24 gr of 3sc/24 x ch7-sp]

In the next Round, make sure to also sk the 3sc-gr between the ch-sps.

R15: Rep Round 9 but the amount of repeats changes to 23 times instead of 11. [24 gr of 7dc]

R16: Rep Round 10 but the amount of repeats changes to 22 times instead of 10. [24 gr of dc2tog-3dc-dc2tog and 24 x ch3-sp]

R17: Rep Round 11 but the amount of repeats changes to 22 times instead of 10. [24 gr of dc2tog-1dc-dc2tog/24pc/48 x ch3-sp]

R18: Rep Round 12 but the amount of repeats changes to 22 times instead of 10. [24 x dc3tog/48pc /72 x ch4-sp]

R19: Rep Round 13 but the amount of repeats changes to 22 times instead of 10. [24dc/72pc/96 x ch3-sp]

HE TOLD ME THINGS ABOUT ME HE COULDN'T KNOW AND ABOUT SOMETHING THAT WOULD HAPPEN IN THE FUTURE

R20: Ss to next ch3-sp. Ch2 (first hdc), 2hdc in same ch3-sp, sk next st. (3hdc in next ch3-sp, sk next st) 95 times. Ss in top of first st to connect. [288hdc]

R21: Ch3 (first dc), 1dc in each st of Round. Ss in top of first st to connect. [288dc]

R22: Ch2 (no st, only used to get to the back of your work), 1bpdc around each st of Round. Ss in top of first st to connect. [288bpdc]

R23: Rep Round 22. [288bpdc]

R24: Ch1, (1sc in next 2 sts, ch5, sk next 2 sts, 1sc in next 2 sts) 48 times. Ss in top of first st to connect. Ss to next ch5-sp. [48 gr of 4sc/48 x ch5-sp]

R25: *Starting in ch5-sp.* Ch1, *1sc-2dc-ch3-2dc-1sc in ch5-sp, sk next st, 1sc in next 2 sts, sk next st. Rep from * 47 more times. Ss in top of first st to connect. Ss to next ch3-sp. [48 fans of 1sc-2dc-ch3-2dc-1sc and 48 gr of 2sc]

R26: *Starting in ch3-sp.* Ch1, *1sc-1dc-ch2-1dc-1sc in ch3-sp, ch5, sk all sts until first sc of next 2sc-gr, 1sc in each of the two sc of the 2sc-gr, ch5, sk all sts to next ch3-sp. Rep from * 47 more times. Ss in top of first st to connect. Ss to next ch2-sp. [48 gr of 1sc-1dc-ch2-1dc-1sc/48 gr of 2sc/96 x ch5-sp]

R27: *Starting in ch2-sp.* Ch1, *1sc-ch3-1sc in ch2-sp, ch4, 2sc in next ch5-sp, sk the next 2 sts, 2sc in next ch5-sp, ch4. Rep from * 47 more times. Ss in top of first st to connect. Suppose you crochet the mandala into a ring – ss to next ch3-sp. If not, fasten off yarn. [48 gr of 1sc-ch3-1sc/48 gr of 4sc/96 x ch4-sp]

If you decide to work your mandala into a ring. Crochet an sc through the ch3-sp and the ring at the same time. Then crochet 7sc around the ring. Now take the next ch3-sp and work sc through it. Repeat attaching a ch3-sp and then working 7sc around the circle until the mandala is fully connected to the ring. Ss in top of first st and fasten off yarn. Weave in all remaining ends.

If you decided not to use a ring, weave in all ends and block your project in a full circle and as wide as possible for the best outcome.

27
26
25
24
23
22
21
20
19
18
17
16
15
14
13
12
11
10
9
8
7
6
5
4
3
2
1

40° 42' N, 74° 0' W
• MANHATTAN • EMPIRE STATE BUILDING
• METRO • BEACH • STATUE OF LIBERTY

USA (NEW YORK)

RAINBOW SUBWAY BLANKET

The most interesting and fun way to get from A to B for me is the metro. Most large cities have built a subway, and they come in different styles. Take one of the most famous—the Tube in London. "Mind your step" will never be the same once you have traveled through the old and classical stations under London. Or the Parisian metro! If you like to take a step back in time and enjoy a traditional French ride, you must buy a metro ticket and take one of the older lines. You might be surprised by musicians entering your carriage and serenading you.

But my number one favorite underground transport is still the New York subway. This network of lines is extensive and prominent and has a great many stations that transport millions of people every day. It is hard not to get lost in the complex network of lines that the New York subway holds. For that reason, I also find it fascinating to see those colorful and yet simple subway maps. For me, it seems like an explosion of colors as each line on the map is represented by a different color. The map simplifies those intricate lines to help you understand how to find your way underground. There is no better experience as a tourist than sitting in a metro just watching daily life passing by. For me, it is an essential part of traveling and helps me to understand a different culture or place. I have tried to capture my fascination with the subway in this blanket. Many rainbow colors are in it, just as in a large metro map with colored lines connecting to each other. I also tried to capture the bending train tracks, which form a nice texture to this blanket.

CROSLEY
WAIKIKI'S

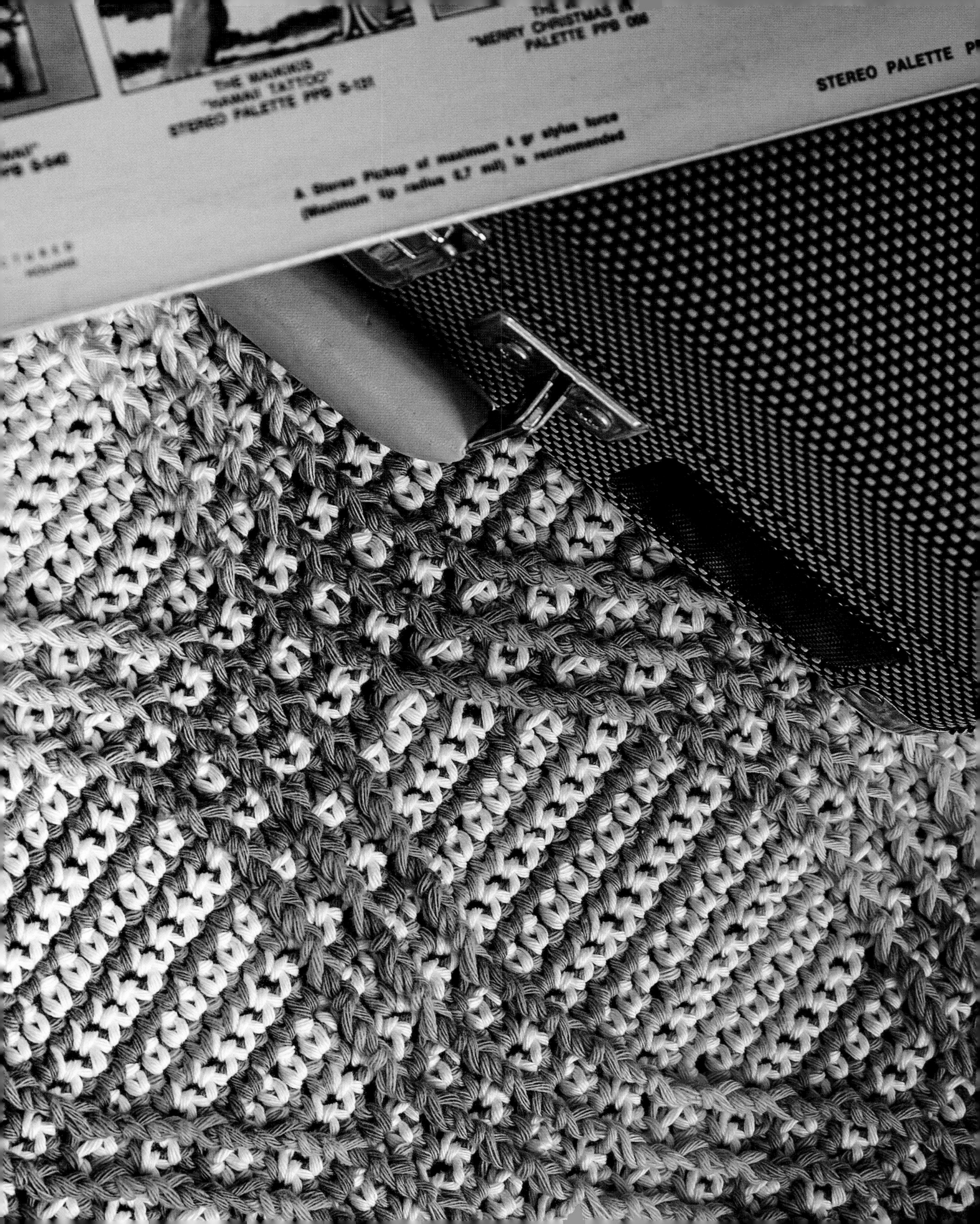
"HAWAII TATTOO"
STEREO PALETTE

PATTERN

With crochet hook size 5.5mm (I/9) and Color A, ch147.

R1 (RS): 1sc in the second ch from hook, 1sc in next 145 ch. Put Color A aside. [146sc]

R2 (RS): Take Color B and attach it to the Row's first st on the work's Right Side. Ch1 (doesn't count as st here and throughout entire pattern), 1sc in first 3 sts, 1sc in blo of next 140 sts, 1sc in last 3 sts. Fasten off Color B. [3sc/140sc in blo/3sc]

R3 (WS): Pick up Color A in the first st of Row on the Wrong Side of the work. Ch1, 1sc in each st of Row. Put Color A aside. [146sc]

HOOK SIZES NEEDED: 5.5MM (I/9) AND 6.0MM (J/10) HOOK SIZE

YARN NEEDED: SCHEEPJES CAHLISTA COMES IN BALLS OF 50G (1¾OZ) WITH A LENGTH OF 85M (93YDS) OF YARN. THE YARN CONSISTS OF 100% NATURAL COTTON.

- 12 BALLS OF SCHEEPJES CAHLISTA – COLOR 106 SNOW WHITE (COLOR A)
- 1 SCHEEPJES CAHLISTA COLOR PACK (COLOR B) – *IF YOU DON'T LIKE TO USE A COLOR PACK, YOU CAN ALSO CHANGE COLOR B FOR JUST ONE COLOR OF YARN OR A GRADIENT-TYPE YARN. YOU MIGHT NEED APPROXIMATELY 2500 METERS (2734YDS) OF YARN FOR COLOR B.*

SIZE OF PROJECT: THE BLANKET WILL HAVE A LENGTH OF 152CM (60IN) AND A WIDTH OF 114CM (45IN).

TIPS FOR THIS PATTERN:

- IN THE PATTERN, YOU WILL USE COLOR A AND B. COLOR A IS A SINGLE WHITE COLOR. COLOR B WILL BE THE COLOR PACK THAT HOLDS 109 COLORS OF YARN. YOU WILL USE 107 COLORS OUT OF THE COLOR PACK. EACH ROW B YOU CROCHET, YOU WILL TAKE A NEW COLOR OUT OF THE COLOR PACK. YOU CAN FOLLOW THE USE OF COLORS IN THE COLOR SCHEDULE. YOU START WITH COLOR 1 AND WORK UNTIL YOU REACH COLOR 107.
- IF YOU DECIDE NOT TO USE A COLOR PACK AS COLOR B BUT JUST A SINGLE COLOR OF YARN, YOU STILL NEED TO ATTACH AND FASTEN OFF THE YARN AT EACH ROW AS THESE ROWS ARE ALL MADE ON THE RIGHT SIDE OF THE WORK.
- EVERY ROW MADE WITH COLOR A WILL BE A ROW OF SINGLE CROCHETS, WHICH CHANGES FROM THE RIGHT SIDE OF THE WORK TO THE WRONG SIDE.
- EVERY ROW MADE WITH COLOR B WILL HAVE TR OR FPTR STITCHES. WHEN YOU MAKE A TR OR AN FPTR, YOU ALWAYS SKIP A STITCH BEHIND IT. THIS IS NOT WRITTEN DOWN INDIVIDUALLY IN THE PATTERN, SO KEEP THIS IN MIND AS YOU WORK.
- THE COLORED SECTION OF THIS PATTERN'S CHART INDICATES THE REPEATING ROWS FOR THIS PATTERN.

R4 (RS): Take Color B and attach it to the Row's first st on the work's Right Side. Ch1, 1sc in first 3 sts, *(1tr in flo of Row 2, 1sc in next st) 3 times, 1sc in next 8 sts, (1tr in flo of Row 2, 1sc in next st) 3 times. Rep from * 6 more times. 1sc in the last 3 sts. Fasten off Color B. [104sc/42tr]

R5 (RS): Pick up Color A in the first st of Row on the Right Side of the work. Ch1, 1sc in each st of Row. Put Color A aside. [146sc]

R6 (RS): Take Color B and attach it to the Row's first st on the work's Right Side. Ch1, 1sc in first 3 sts, *(1sc in next st, 1fptr around next tr you just passed of Row 4) 3 times, 1sc in next 7 sts, (1fptr around next tr of Row 4, 1sc in next st) 3 times, 1sc in next st. Rep from * 6 more times. 1sc in the last 3 sts. Fasten off Color B. [104sc/42fptr]

THIS NETWORK OF LINES IS SO EXTENSIVE AND PROMINENT AND HAS MANY STATIONS THAT TRANSPORT MILLIONS OF PEOPLE DAILY

R7 (WS): Pick up Color A in the first st of Row on the Wrong Side of the work. Ch1, 1sc in each st of Row. Put Color A aside. [146sc]

R8 (RS): Take Color B and attach it to the Row's first st on the work's Right Side. Ch1, 1sc in first 3 sts, *1sc in next st, (1sc in next st, 1fptr around next fptr you just passed two Rows down) 3 times, 1sc in next 5 sts, (1fptr around next fptr two Rows down, 1sc in next st) 3 times, 1sc in next 2 sts. Rep from * 6 more times. 1sc in the last 3 sts. Fasten off Color B. [104sc/42fptr]

R9 (RS): Pick up Color A in the first st of Row on the Right Side of the work. Ch1, 1sc in each st of Row. Put Color A aside. [146sc]

R10 (RS): Take Color B and attach it to the Row's first st on the work's Right Side. Ch1, 1sc in first 3 sts, *1sc in next 2 sts, (1sc in next st, 1fptr around next fptr you just passed two Rows down) 3 times, 1sc in next 3 sts, (1fptr around next fptr two Rows down, 1sc in next st) 3 times, 1sc in next 3 sts. Rep from * 6 more times. 1sc in the last 3 sts. Fasten off Color B. [104sc/42fptr]

R11 (WS): Pick up Color A in the first st of Row on the Wrong Side of the work. Ch1, 1sc in each st of Row. Put Color A aside. [146sc]

R12 (RS): Take Color B and attach it to the Row's first st on the work's Right Side. Ch1, 1sc in first 3 sts, *1sc in next 3 sts, (1sc in next st, 1fptr around next fptr you just passed two Rows down) 3 times, 1sc in next st, (1fptr around next fptr two Rows down, 1sc in next st) 3 times, 1sc in next 4 sts. Rep from * 6 more times. 1sc in the last 3 sts. Fasten off Color B. [104sc/42fptr]

R13 (RS): Pick up Color A in the first st of Row on the Right Side of the work. Ch1, 1sc in each st of Row. Put Color A aside. [146sc]

R14 (RS): Take Color B and attach it to the Row's first st on the work's Right Side. Ch1, 1sc in first 3 sts, *1sc in next 3 sts, (1sc in next st, 1fptr around next fptr two Rows down) 3 times, 1sc in next st, (1fptr around next fptr two Rows down, 1sc in next st) 3 times, 1sc in next 4 sts. Rep from * 6 more times. 1sc in the last 3 sts. [104sc/42fptr]

R15 (WS): Pick up Color A in the first st of Row on the Wrong Side of the work. Ch1, 1sc in each st of Row. Put Color A aside. [146sc]

R16 (RS): Rep Row 14. [104sc/42fptr]

R17 (RS): Pick up Color A in the first st of Row on the Right Side of the work. Ch1, 1sc in each st of Row. Put Color A aside. [146sc]

I TRIED TO CAPTURE THE BENDING TRAIN TRACKS, WHICH GIVE A NICE TEXTURE TO THIS BLANKET

1	383 Ginger gold
2	179 Topaz
3	502 Camel
4	404 English Tea
5	130 Old Lace
6	509 Baby Blue
7	173 Bluebell
8	510 Sky Blue
9	247 Bluebird
10	261 Capri Blue
11	508 Deep Amethyst
12	164 Light Navy
13	244 Spruce
14	525 Fir
15	391 Deep Ocean
16	401 Dark Teal
17	400 Petrol Blue
18	514 Jade
19	241 Parrot Green
20	253 Tropic
21	528 Silver Blue
22	402 Silver Green
23	172 Light Silver
24	238 Powder pink
25	246 Icy Pink
26	222 Tulip
27	519 Freesia

R18 (RS): Rep Row 14. [104sc/42fptr]

R19 (WS): Pick up Color A in the first st of Row on the Wrong Side of the work. Ch1, 1sc in each st of Row. Put Color A aside. [146sc]

R20 (RS): Take Color B and attach it to the Row's first st on the work's Right Side. Ch1, 1sc in first 3 sts, *1sc in next 2 sts, (1sc in next st, 1fptr around next fptr two Rows down) 3 times, 1sc in next 3 sts, (1fptr around

28	114 Shocking Pink	55	526 Ashes	82	212 Sage Green
29	256 Cornelia Rose	56	394 Shadow Purple	83	395 Willow
30	115 Hot Red	57	517 Ruby	84	254 Moon Rock
31	390 Poppy Rose	58	192 Scarlet	85	406 Soft Beige
32	516 Candy Apple	59	258 Rosewood	86	248 Champagne
33	252 Watermelon	60	413 Cherry	87	505 Linen
34	410 Rich Coral	61	251 Garden Rose	88	105 Bridal White
35	386 Peach	62	128 Tyrian Purple	89	101 Candlelight
36	524 Apricot	63	282 Ultra Violet	90	100 Lemon Chiffon
37	414 Vintage Peach	64	113 Delphinium	91	403 Lemonade
38	263 Petal Peach	65	521 Deep Violet	92	522 Primrose
39	257 Antique Mauve	66	527 Midnight	93	280 Lemon
40	506 Caramel	67	124 Ultramarine	94	249 Saffron
41	503 Hazelnut	68	201 Electric Blue	95	208 Yellow Gold
42	157 Root beer	69	511 Cornflower	96	411 Sweet Orange
43	507 Chocolate	70	384 Powder Blue	97	281 Tangerine
44	162 Black Coffee	71	146 Vivid Blue	98	189 Royal Orange
45	393 Charcoal	72	397 Cyan	99	388 Rust
46	387 Dark Olive	73	385 Crystalline	100	504 Brick Red
47	501 Anthracite	74	392 Lime Juice	101	396 Rose Wine
48	242 Metal Grey	75	245 Green Yellow	102	409 Soft Rose
49	074 Mercury	76	512 Lime	103	264 Light Coral
50	399 Lilac Mist	77	205 Kiwi	104	518 Marshmallow
51	226 Light Orchid	78	513 Apple Granny	105	408 Old Rose
52	520 Lavender	79	412 Forest Green	106	523 Sweet Mandarin
53	398 Coral Rose	80	389 Apple Green	107	255 Shell
54	240 Amethyst	81	515 Emerald		

next fptr you just passed two Rows down, 1sc in next st) 3 times, 1sc in next 3 sts. Rep from * 6 more times. 1sc in the last 3 sts. Fasten off Color B. [104sc/42fptr]

R21 (RS): Pick up Color A in the first st of Row on the Right Side of the work. Ch1, 1sc in each st of Row. Put Color A aside. [146sc]

R22 (RS): Take Color B and attach it to the Row's first st on the work's Right Side. Ch1, 1sc in first 3 sts, *1sc in next st, (1sc in next st, 1fptr around next fptr two Rows down) 3 times, 1sc in next 5 sts, (1fptr around next fptr you just passed two Rows down, 1sc in next st) 3 times, 1sc in next 2 sts. Rep from * 6 more times. 1sc in the last 3 sts. Fasten off Color B. [104sc/42fptr]

R23 (WS): Pick up Color A in the first st of Row on the Wrong Side of the work. Ch1, 1sc in each st of Row. Put Color A aside. [146sc]

R24 (RS): Take Color B and attach it to the Row's first st on the work's Right Side. Ch1, 1sc in first 3 sts, *(1sc in next st, 1fptr around next fptr two Rows down) 3 times, 1sc in next 7 sts, (1fptr around next fptr you just passed two Rows down, 1sc in next st) 3 times, 1sc in next st. Rep from * 6 more times. 1sc in the last 3 sts. Fasten off Color B. [104sc/42fptr]

R25 (RS): Pick up Color A in the first st of Row on the Right Side of the work. Ch1, 1sc in each st of Row. Put Color A aside. [146sc]

R26 (RS): Take Color B and attach it to the Row's first st on the work's Right Side. Ch1, 1sc in first 3 sts, *(1fptr around next fptr two Rows down, 1sc in next st) 3 times, 1sc in next 8 sts, (1fptr around next fptr you just passed two Rows down, 1sc in next st) 3 times. Rep from * 6 more times. 1sc in the last 3 sts. Fasten off Color B. [104sc/42tr]

R27 (WS): Pick up Color A in the first st of Row on the Wrong Side of the work. Ch1, 1sc in each st of Row. Put Color A aside. [146sc]

R28 (RS): Take Color B and attach it to the Row's first st on the work's Right Side. Ch1, 1sc in first 3 sts, *(1fptr around next fptr two Rows down, 1sc in next st) 3 times, 1sc in next 8 sts, (1fptr around next fptr two Rows down, 1sc in next st) 3 times. Rep from * 6 more times. 1sc in the last 3 sts. Fasten off Color B. [104sc/42tr]

R29 (RS): Pick up Color A in the first st of Row on the Right Side of the work. Ch1, 1sc in each st of Row. Put Color A aside. [146sc]

R30 (RS): Rep Row 28. [104sc/42fptr]

R31 (WS): Pick up Color A in the first st of Row on the Wrong Side of the work. Ch1, 1sc in each st of Row. Put Color A aside. [146sc]

R32 (RS): Rep Row 28. [104sc/42fptr]

R33 (RS): Pick up Color A in the first st of Row on the Right Side of the work. Ch1, 1sc in each st of Row. Put Color A aside. [146sc]

R34 (RS): Rep Row 28. [104sc/42fptr]

R35 (WS): Pick up Color A in the first st of Row on the Wrong Side of the work. Ch1, 1sc in each st of Row. Put Color A aside. [146sc]

R36 (RS): Take Color B and attach it to the Row's first st on the work's Right Side. Ch1, 1sc in first 3 sts, *(1sc in next st, 1fptr around next fptr you just passed two Rows down) 3 times, 1sc in next 7 sts, (1fptr around next fptr two Rows down, 1sc in next st) 3 times, 1sc in next st. Rep from * 6 more times. 1sc in the last 3 sts. Fasten off Color B. [104sc/42fptr]

R37 (RS): Pick up Color A in the first st of Row on the Right Side of the work. Ch1, 1sc in each st of Row. Put Color A aside. [146sc]

Now repeat **Rows 8-37** another 5 times. Once you've completed that, repeat **Rows 8-35** once more. You will now have used all the 107 colors out of the color list. Fasten off Color A and weave in all ends.

Border Rows:
Take crochet hook size 6.0mm (J/10) and Color A, attach it in the first st of the last Row on the Right Side of the work.

R1 (RS): Ch1, 1sc in first 2 sts, (ch1, sk next st, 1sc in next st) 72 times. Turn work. [74sc/72 x ch1-sp]

R2 (WS): Ch1, 1sc in first st, (1sc in next ch1-sp, ch1, sk next st) 72 times, 1sc in last st. Turn work. [74sc/72 x ch1-sp]

R3–9: Rep Row 2. [74sc/72 x ch1-sp]
Fasten off Color A and weave in the remaining ends.

Repeat these Border Rows at the opposite side of the blanket. It means the blanket will have a border at the top and bottom. Block the blanket for the best outcome.

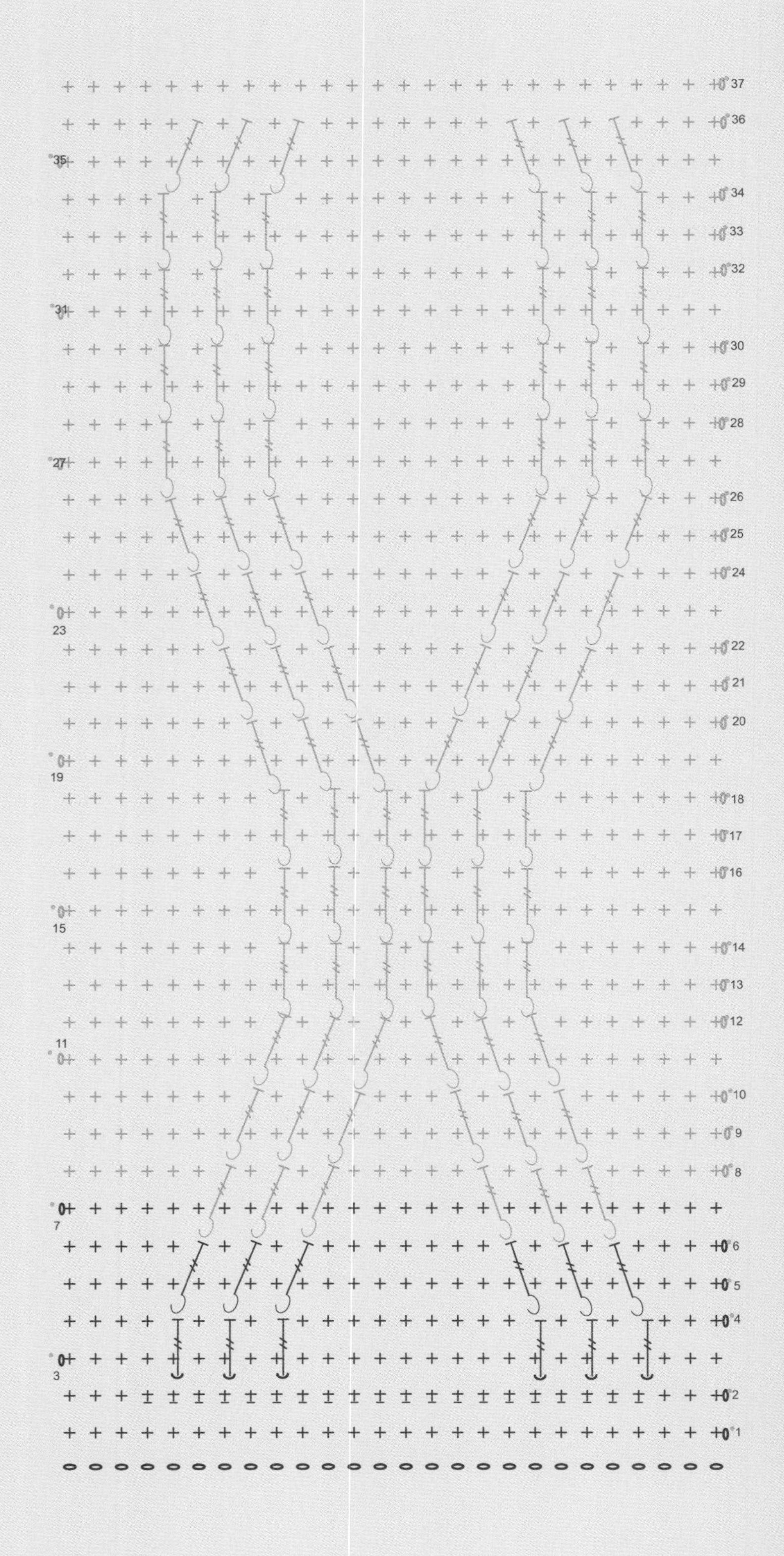

37
36
35
34
33
32
31
30
29
28
27
26
25
24
23
22
21
20
19
18
17
16
15
14
13
12
11
10
9
8
7
6
5
4
3
2
1

34° 36′ S, 58° 22′ W
• RÍO DE LA PLATA • LA BOCA
• TANGO • DANCING • METROPOLIS

ARGENTINA
(BUENOS AIRES)

LA BOCA SHAWL

For this story and pattern, we travel to South America, to the capital of Argentina to be exact. Buenos Aires is a large city that could take weeks or even months to wander around. But there is one area in the town which is my favorite—La Boca. This region of Buenos Aires started out as a harbor entrance for trading in the early days. People from all over the world gathered to work or live around the harbor. The working class started collecting scraps of metal, paint, and other materials from the shipments that arrived in the port and from these scraps, they built an entire neighborhood, and so La Boca came to life. You will find houses in all colors of the rainbow, and it gives you a happy feeling when you take a walk around. A good suggestion is walking the "little path," where you see brightly colored buildings—the result of lots of leftover paint. When wandering around in La Boca, it is hard not to let your attention be drawn by the Tango dancers. You can hear the sound of Tango music on almost every corner and with it, you often find a pair of dancers in a passionate dance. It is fascinating to see, and although it is done to draw in as many tourists as possible, it lifts your spirits.
It is lovely to sit down at one of the local bars, order a dulce de leche with a Fernet con coca, taste the local food and drink, and enjoy the whole ambience around you. It is just one of the amazing things Buenos Aires has to offer—of course, there is so much more, but this particular area stole my heart.
This triangular shawl is inspired by the feminine Tango dancer, who often wears a lace shawl around her shoulders. Combined with an explosion of colors that you can find almost everywhere in La Boca, this pattern was the result.

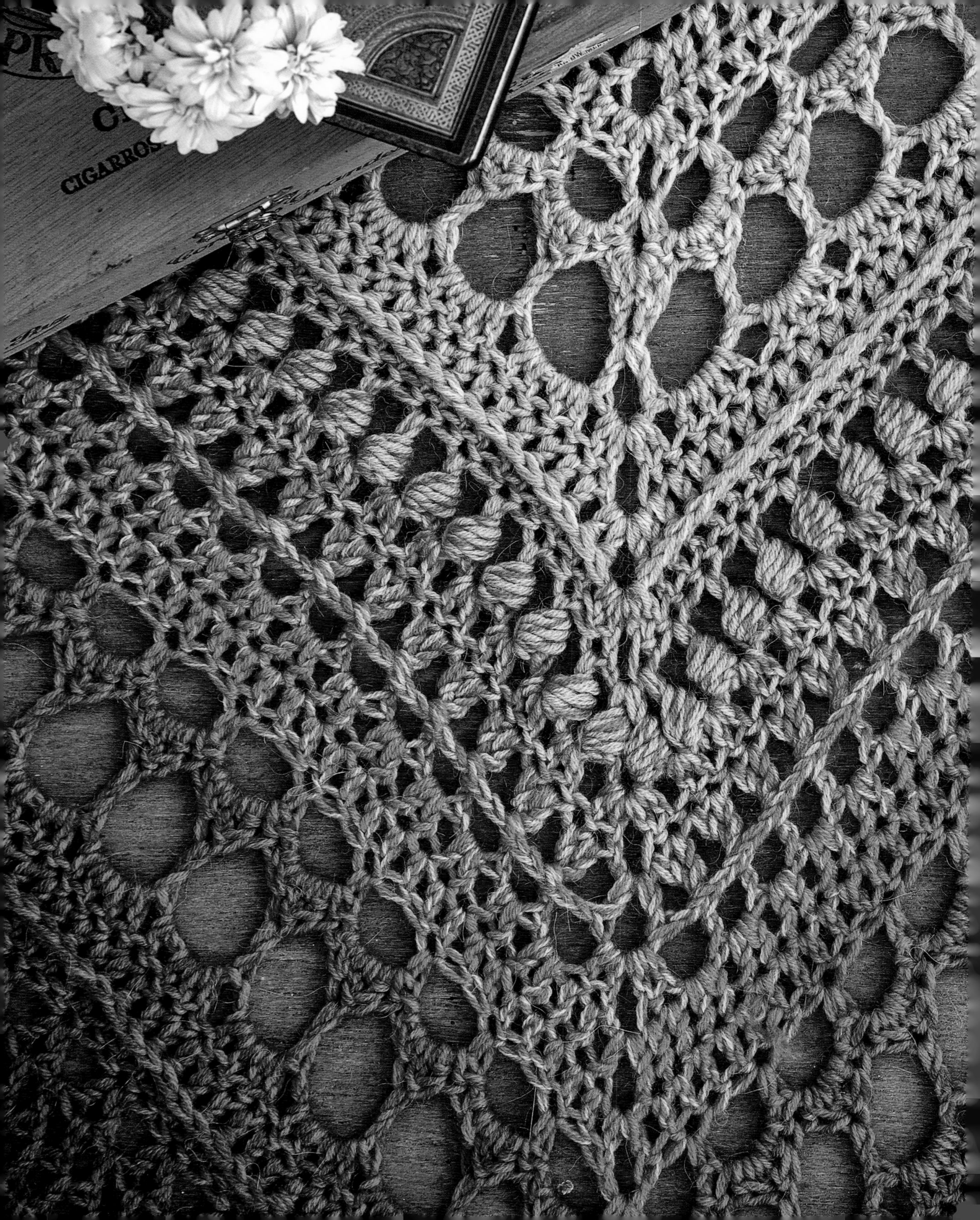
CIGARROS

PATTERN

With a 5.5mm (I/9) crochet hook and the yarn, make a ML.

R1 (WS): Ch3 (first dc), 2dc-ch3-3dc in same loop. Turn. [2 sides of 3dc and a ch3-top]

R2 (RS): Ch3 (first dc), 1dc in same st, 1dc in next 2 sts, 2dc-ch3-2dc in next ch3-top, 1dc in next 2 sts, 2dc in last st. Turn. [2 sides of 6dc and a ch3-top]

R3 (WS): Ch4 (first dc + ch1), 1dc in same st, (ch1, sk next st, 1dc in next st) 2 times, ch1, sk next st, 2dc-ch3-2dc in next ch3-top, (ch1, sk next st, 1dc in next st) 2 times, ch1 , sk next st, 1dc-ch1-1dc in last st. Turn. [2 sides of 6dc/4 x ch1-sp and a ch3-top]

R4 (RS): Ch3 (first dc), 1dc in same st, 1dc in each st and ch1-sp on the side to next ch3-top, 1dc-ch3-1dc in next ch3-top, 1dc in each st and ch1-sp to last st on the side, 2dc in last st *(which will be the third ch of the ch4 you started with the previous Row)* Turn. [2 sides of 12dc and a ch3-top]

R5 (WS): Ch3 (first dc), 1dc in same st, 1dc in each st of side to next ch3-top, 2dc-ch3-2dc in next ch3-top, 1dc in each st of side to last st, 2dc in last st. Turn. [2 sides of 15dc and a ch3-top]

R6 (RS): Ch4 (first dc + ch1), 1dc in same st, 1puff st around the dc you just made, (ch1, sk next st, 1dc in next st, 1puff st around the dc you just created) to next ch3-top,ch1, 1dc in next ch3-top, 1puff st around the dc you just made, ch3, 1dc in the same ch3-top, 1puff st around the dc you just made, ch1, (1dc in next st, 1 puff st around the dc you just made, ch1, sk next st) to last st on the side, 1dc in last st, 1puff st around the dc you just made, ch1, 1dc in same last st. Turn. [2 sides of 1dc/9dc with a puff st around it/9 x ch1-sp and a ch3-top]

In the next Row, you skip all the puff sts.

R7 (WS): Ch3 (first dc), 1dc in same st, (2dc in next ch1-sp) to next ch3-top, 2dc-ch3-2dc in next ch3-top, (2dc in next ch1-sp) to last st, 2dc in last st. Turn. [2 sides of 2dc/ 10 x 2dc-gr and a ch3-top]

HOOK SIZE NEEDED: 5.5MM (I/9) HOOK

YARN NEEDED: 1 SCHEEPJES WHIRLIGIG COLOR 210 PLUM TO OCHRE, WHICH COMES IN CAKES OF 450G (16OZ) WITH A LENGTH OF 997M (1090YDS) OF YARN. THE YARN CONSISTS OF 20% ALPACA/ 80% VIRGIN WOOL.

SIZE OF PROJECT: THE SHAWL HAS A TRIANGULAR SHAPE. AFTER BLOCKING, THE LONGEST SIDE WILL BE APPROX. 165CM (65IN), THE TWO SMALLER SIDES WILL BE AROUND 130CM (52IN) LONG, AND THE DEPTH OF THE SHAWL WILL BE ABOUT 100CM (39IN).

TIPS FOR THIS PATTERN:

- THE PATTERN IS WORKED IN ROWS WHICH MEANS YOU WILL TURN BETWEEN THE RIGHT SIDE AND THE WRONG SIDE.
- THE PATTERN HAS A LOT OF OPEN SPACES AND A BIT OF A LACE LOOK. FOR THIS REASON, THE SHAWL WILL GET OUT OF SHAPE WHILE CROCHETING THE ROWS. IT ALSO MEANS THE SHAWL NEEDS A REAL TIGHT BLOCKING ONCE FINISHED. THE BEST WAY TO DO THIS IS TO LET THE SHAWL SOAK IN

R8 (RS): Ch3 (first dc), 1dc in same st, sk next st, (ch2, 1dc2tog over next 2dc-gr) to next ch3-top, ch2, 1dc-ch3-1dc in next ch3-top, (ch2, 1dc2tog over next 2dc-gr) to last 2 sts, ch2, sk next st, 2dc in last st. Turn. [2 sides of 3dc/10 x dc2tog/11 x ch2-sp and a ch3-top]

R9 (WS): Ch3 (first dc), 1dc in same st, 1dc in next st, (ch2, 1fpdc around next dc2tog) to last dc on side, ch2, sk next dc, 2dc-ch3-2dc in next ch3-top, ch2, sk next dc, (1fpdc around next dc2tog, ch2) to last 2 sts on side, 1dc in next st, 2dc in last st. Turn. [2 sides of 5dc/10fpdc/11 x ch2-sp and a ch3-top]

R10 (RS): Ch3 (first dc), 1dc in same st, 1dc in next 2 sts (2dc in next ch2-sp, sk next st) to last ch2-sp on side, 2dc in next ch2-sp, 1dc in next 2 sts, 1dc-ch3-1dc in next ch3-top, 1dc in next 2 sts, (2dc in next ch2-sp, sk next st) to last ch2-sp on side, 2dc in next ch2-sp, 1dc in next 2 sts, 2dc in last st. Turn. [2 sides of 29dc and a ch3-top]

R11 (WS): Ch3 (first dc), 1dc in same st, 1dc in each st to next ch3-top, 2dc-ch3-2dc in next ch3-top, 1dc in each st to last st, 2dc in last st. Turn. [2 sides of 32dc and a ch3-top]

R12 (RS): Ch6 (first dc + ch3), sk next st, (1sc in next st, ch5, sk next 2 sts) to next ch3-top, 1sc-ch3-1sc in next ch3-top, (ch5, sk next 2 sts, 1sc in next st) to last 2 sts on side, ch3, sk next st, 1dc in last st. Turn. [2 sides of 11sc/1dc/1 x ch3-sp/10 x ch5-sp and a ch3-top]

R13 (WS): Ch3 (first dc), 1dc-1hdc-1sc in next ch3-sp, sk next st, (1sc-1hdc-1dc-1hdc-1sc in next ch5-sp, sk next st) to next ch3-top, 1sc-1hdc-1dc-ch3-1dc-1hdc-1sc in next ch3-top, sk next st, (1sc-1hdc-1dc-1hdc-1sc in next ch5-sp, sk next st) to last ch3-sp on side, 1sc-1hdc-1dc in next ch3-sp, 1dc in last st *(which will be the third ch of the ch6 you began with last Row)*. Turn. [2 sides of 1dc/1 half fan of 1dc-1hdc-1sc/10 fans of 1sc-1hdc-1dc-1hdc-1sc/1 half fan of 1sc-1hdc-1dc and a ch3-top]

R14 (RS): Ch3 (first dc), 1dc in same st, (ch5, sk all sts to next dc of a whole fan, 1dc in dc) up to last whole fan on the side, ch5, sk all sts up till next ch3-top, 1dc-ch3-1dc in next ch3-top, (ch5, sk all sts to next dc of whole fan, 1dc in dc) to last whole fan on the side, ch5, sk all sts to last st on the side, 2dc in last st. Turn. [2 sides of 13dc/11 x ch5-sp and a ch3-top]

WATER, WRING IT OUT AND BLOCK IT AT EACH POINT OF THE SHAWL.

- THE PATTERN IS CROCHETED WITH A 5.5MM (I/9) HOOK SIZE; I CHOSE TO GIVE THE SHAWL ENOUGH DRAPE TO WEAR IT WITHOUT HAVING TOO MUCH TENSION IN THE DESIGN. IF YOU CROCHET PRETTY LOOSE, I WOULD SUGGEST USING ONE SIZE SMALLER.
- IN THE PATTERN, I MENTION A CH-TOP. IT IS THE CH-SP BETWEEN THE TWO SIDES. THE PATTERN WILL REFER TO THIS TOP TO MARK THE POINT WHERE YOU ARE IN A ROW.
- IN THE PATTERN, YOU WILL FIND A LOT OF SHORT REPEAT SECTIONS IN THE ROWS. THE REPEAT SECTION MUST BE REPEATED OVER THE ENTIRE SIDE TO THE NEXT ST, WHICH IS GIVEN AFTER THE REPEAT SECTION.
- THE CHART OF THIS PATTERN SHOWS ROUNDS 1-17. ROUNDS 18-40 ARE NOT CHARTED BECAUSE THESE ARE JUST REPEATING ROUNDS FROM ROUNDS 1-17. ROUNDS 41-49 ARE CHARTED WITH A NUMBER OF REPEATS TO SHOW WHAT THESE ROUNDS WILL LOOK LIKE.

R15 (WS): Ch3 (first dc), 1dc in same st, 1dc in next st, (4dc in next ch5-sp, sk next st) to next ch3-top, 2dc-ch3-2dc in next ch3-top, (sk next st, 4dc in next ch5-sp) to last 2 sts on side, 1dc in next st, 2dc in last st. Turn. [2 sides of 49dc and a ch3-top]

R16 (RS): Ch3 (first dc), 1dc in same st, 1dc in each st to next ch3-top, 2dc-ch3-2dc in next ch3-top, 1dc in each st to last st, 2dc in last st. Turn. [2 sides of 52dc and a ch3-top]

R17 (WS): Ch3 (first dc), 1dc in same st, 1fpdc around each st on side to next ch3-top, 2dc-ch3-2dc in next ch3-top, 1fpdc around each st on side to last st on side, 2dc in last st. Turn. [2 sides of 4dc/51fpdc and a ch3-top]

R18 (RS): Rep Row 6. [2 sides of 1dc/ 29dc with a puff st around it/29 x ch1-sp and a ch3-top]

R19 (WS): Rep Row 7. [2 sides of 2dc/30 x 2dc-gr and a ch3-top]

R20 (RS): Rep Row 8. [2 sides of 3dc/30 x dc2tog/31 x ch2-sp and a ch3-top]

R21 (WS): Rep Row 9. [2 sides of 5dc/30fpdc/31 x ch2-sp and a ch3-top]

R22 (RS): Rep Row 10. [2 sides of 69dc and a ch3-top]

R23 (WS): Ch3 (first dc), 1dc in same st, 1dc in each st to next ch3-top, 1dc-ch3-1dc in next ch3-top, 1dc in each st to last st, 2dc in last st. Turn. [2 sides of 71dc and a ch3-top]

R24 (RS): Rep Row 12. [2 sides of 24sc/1dc/1 x ch3-sp/23 x ch5-sp and a ch3-top]

R25 (WS): Rep Row 13. [2 sides of 1dc/1 half fan of 1dc-1hdc-1sc/23 fans of 1sc-1hdc-1dc-1hdc-1sc/1 half fan of 1sc-1hdc-1dc and a ch3-top]

R26 (RS): Rep Row 14. [2 sides of 26dc/24 x ch5-sp and a ch3-top]

R27 (WS): Rep Row 15. [2 sides of 101dc and a ch3-top]

R28 (RS): Rep Row 16. [2 sides of 104dc and a ch3-top]

R29 (WS): Rep Row 17. [2 sides of 4dc/103fpdc and a ch3-top]

R30 (RS): Rep Row 6. [2 sides of 1dc/ 55dc with a puff st around it/55 x ch1-sp and a ch3-top]

R31 (WS): Rep Row 7. [2 sides of 2dc/56 x 2dc-gr and a ch3-top]

R32 (RS): Rep Row 8. [2 sides of 3dc/56 x dc2tog/57 x ch2-sp and a ch3-top]

R33 (WS): Rep Row 9. [2 sides of 5dc/56fpdc/57 x ch2-sp and a ch3-top]

R34 (RS): Rep Row 10. [2 sides of 121dc and a ch3-top]

R35 (WS): Ch3 (first dc), 1dc in each st up till next ch3-top, 1dc-ch3-1dc in next ch3-top, 1dc in each st up till last st, 1dc in last st. Turn. [2 sides of 122dc and a ch3-top]

R36 (RS): Rep Row 12. [2 sides of 41sc/1dc/1 x ch3-sp/40 x ch5-sp and a ch3-top]

R37 (WS): Rep Row 13. [2 sides of 1dc/1 half fan of 1dc-1hdc-1sc/40 fans of 1sc-1hdc-1dc-1hdc-1sc/1 half fan of 1sc-1hdc-1dc and a ch3-top]

R38 (RS): Rep Row 14. [2 sides of 43dc/41 x ch5-sp and a ch3-top]

R39 (WS): Rep Row 15. [2 sides of 169dc and a ch3-top]

R40 (RS): Rep Row 16. [2 sides of 172dc and a ch3-top]

R41 (WS): Rep Row 17. [2 sides of 4dc/171fpdc and a ch3-top]

R42 (RS): Ch4 (first dc + ch1), 1dc in same st, sk next 2 sts, (1dc-ch1-1dc in next st, sk next 2 sts) to the last st on this side, sk 1 st, 1dc-ch1-1dc in next ch3-top, ch3, 1dc-ch1-1dc in same ch3-top, sk 1 st, (sk next 2 sts, 1dc-ch1-1dc in next st) over entire side. Turn. [2 sides of 59 gr of 1dc-ch1-1dc and a ch3-top]

R43 (WS): Ch4 (first dc + ch1), 1dc in next ch1-sp, sk next st, ch1, (1dc between two dc-gr, ch1, sk next st, 1dc in next ch1-sp, ch1, sk next st) to next ch3-top, 1dc-ch3-1dc in next ch3-top, (ch1, sk next st, 1dc in next ch1-sp, ch1, sk next st, 1dc between two dc-gr) to last dc-gr, ch1, sk next st, 1dc in next ch1-sp, ch1, 1dc in last st. Turn. [2 sides of 119dc/118 x ch1-sp and a ch3-top]

R44 (RS): Ch4 (first dc + ch1), 1dc in next ch1-sp, (ch1, sk next st, 1dc in next ch1-sp) to last st on side, ch1, sk next st, 1dc-ch3-1dc in next ch3-top, (ch1, sk next st, 1dc in next ch1-sp) to last st on side, ch1, 1dc in last st. Turn. [2 sides of 120dc/119 x ch1-sp and a ch3-top]

In the next Row, you will only work in the ch1-sps.

R45 (WS): Ch5 (first dc + ch2), 1dc in next ch1-sp, (ch4, 1dc2tog over next two ch1-sps) to next ch3-top, ch4, 1dc-ch3-1dc in next ch3-top, (ch4, 1dc2tog over next two ch1-sps) to last ch1-sp on side, ch4, 1dc in last ch1-sp, ch2, 1dc in last st. Turn. [2 sides of 3dc/1 x ch2-sp/59 x dc2tog/60 x ch4-sp and a ch3-top

R46 (RS): Ch1 (doesn't count as st here and throughout next Rows), 1sc in first st, 3sc in next ch2-sp, (sk next st, 5sc in next ch4-sp) to last st on the side, sk next st, 3sc-ch3-3sc in next ch3-top, (sk next st, 5sc in next ch4-sp) to the last ch2-sp on the side, sk next st, 3sc in next ch2-sp, 1sc in last st. *(which will be the third ch of the ch5 at the start of the last Row)*. Turn. [2 sides of 1sc/2 x 3sc-gr/60 x 5sc-gr and a ch3-top]

R47 (WS): Ch1, 1sc in first st, 1sc in next 2 sts, sk next st, (sk next st, 1sc in next st - *will be the second sc of a 5sc-gr*, 1sc-ch3-1sc in next st, 1sc in next st, sk next st) to the last 3sc-gr on the side, sk next st, 1sc in next 2 sts, 1sc-ch3-1sc in next ch3-top, 1sc in next 2 sts, sk next st, (sk next st, 1sc in next st, 1sc-ch3-1sc in next st, 1sc in next st, sk next st) to the last 3sc-gr on the side, sk next st, 1sc in next 2 sts, 1sc in last st. Turn. [2 sides of 6sc/60 x gr of 2sc-ch3-2sc and a ch3-top]

R48 (RS): Ch1, 1sc in first st, ch6, sk all sts up till next ch3-sp, (1sc in next ch3-sp, ch6, sk all sts to next ch3-sp) to next ch3-top, 1sc-ch6-1sc in next ch3-top, (ch6, sk all sts to next ch3-sp, 1sc in next ch3-sp) to last ch3-sp on side, ch6, sk all sts to last st on side, 1sc in last st. Turn. [2 sides of 62sc/61 x ch6-sp and a ch6-top]

R49 (WS): Ch1, 1sc in first st, (3sc-ch3-3c in next ch6-sp, sk next st) to next ch6-top, 4sc-ch3-4sc in next ch6-top, (sk next st, 3sc-ch3-3sc in next ch6-sp) to last st on side, 1sc in last st. Fasten off yarn. [2 sides of 5sc/61 gr of 3sc-ch3-3sc and a ch3-top]

Weave in ends and block the shawl for the best outcome.

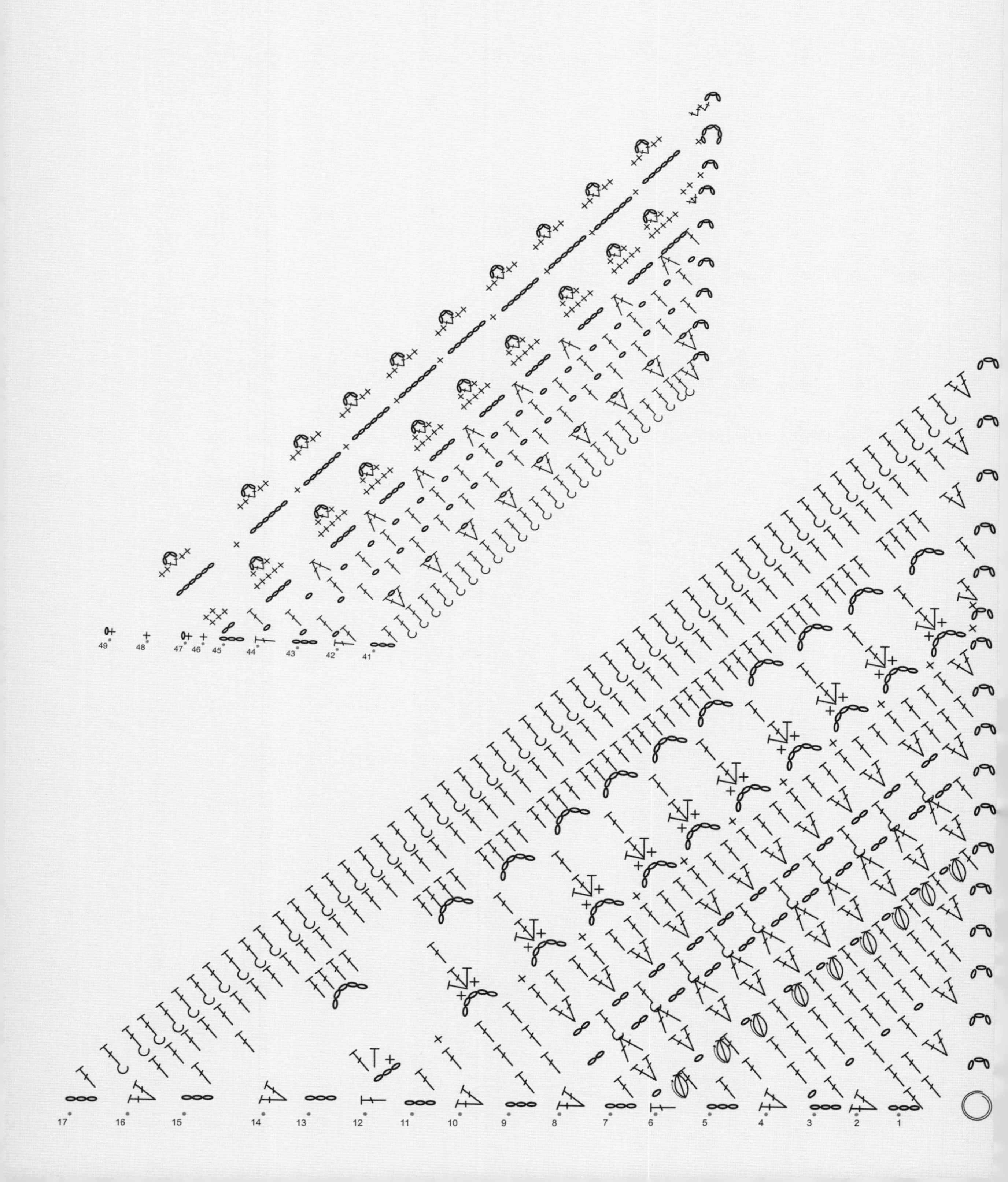
49
48
47
46
45
44
43
42
41
17
16
15
14
13
12
11
10
9
8
7
6
5
4
3
2
1

WHEN WANDERING
AROUND IN LA BOCA,
IT IS HARD NOT TO
LET YOUR ATTENTION
BE DRAWN AWAY
BY TANGO DANCERS

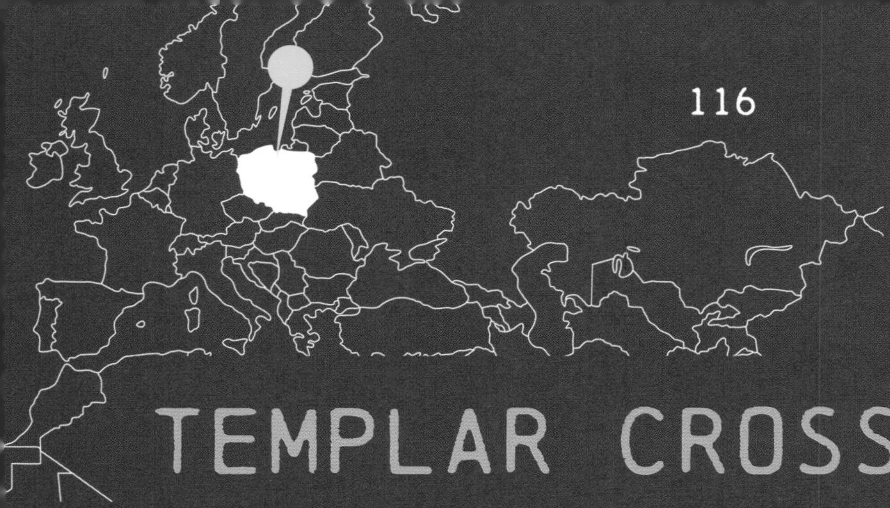

54° 2' N, 19° 1' E
• MIDDLE AGES • SYMBOLS
• CASTLE • CROSS • KNIGHTS

POLAND (MALBORK)

TEMPLAR CROSS TABLE RUNNER

This pattern evolved from a travel story on a trip to Poland. But it could easily have been from England, France, Jerusalem, or Spain as this pattern is inspired by medieval symbols and history, which are found in many countries. But let's get to the story in Malbork first. In Malbork – a small city in Poland, you will find the Teutonic Order's castle. The largest castle ever built and a UNESCO world heritage site, this castle was one of the headquarters in the early days of the Templar Knights: an order of knights who held Christian beliefs and protected all those with the same beliefs. They looked after churches, Christian villages, and fought wars against other religions. We have seen movies or have read books about these times. A good example might be the Knights of the Round table from the stories about Merlin. These knights had different orders in different lands, and they gathered in gigantic fortresses and castles which they owned. There are many castles to see in Poland, but the Malbork castle is one of the largest. It is such a great experience to walk among the old chambers and feel the ancient stone walls which saw incredible historical times. Inside, you will find many old relics and items that remind you of this castle's history—one of these is the Crusader's cross, which is on many decorations and precious items. It was the national symbol of the knight's orders, and we still recognize it today. Nowadays, we might see it mostly on medals without even knowing its history. This cross inspired me to create a design to represent it, which resulted in this beautiful table runner, and with a thinner thread it could also easily be turned into a lovely scarf.

PATTERN

With crochet hook size 4.0mm (G/6) and the Color A, ch69.

R1 (WS): 1sc in the second ch from hook, 1sc in next 67ch. Turn. [68sc]

R2 (RS): 1sc in each st of Row. Turn. [68sc]

R3 (WS): 1sc in each st of Row. Put Color A aside. Turn work. [68sc]

R4 (RS): Take Color B and attach it in first st on Row at Right Side of work. Ch1 (doesn't count as st here and throughout entire pattern), 1sc in next 2 sts, *1sc in next 6 sts, ch1, sk next st, 1sc in next 2 sts, ch1, sk next st, 1sc in next 6 sts. Rep from * 3 more times. 1sc in next 2 sts. Turn. [60sc/8 x ch1-sp]

R5 (WS): 1sc in next 2 sts, *1sc in next 6 sts, ch1, sk next ch1-sp, 1sc in next 2 sts, ch1, sk next ch1-sp, 1sc in next 6 sts. Rep from * 3 more times. 1sc in next 2 sts. Put Color B aside. Turn work. [60sc/8 x ch1-sp]

<u>HOOK SIZE NEEDED:</u> 4.0MM (G/6) AND A 4.5MM (G7) HOOK

<u>YARN NEEDED:</u> SCHEEPJES MERINO SOFT COMES IN BALLS OF 50G (1¾OZ) WITH A LENGTH OF 105M (114YDS) OF YARN. THE YARN CONSISTS OF 50% SUPERWASH MERINO WOOL/25% MICROFIBER/25% ACRYLIC.

- 5 BALLS OF SCHEEPJES MERION SOFT – COLOR 600 MALEVICH (COLOR A)
- 1 BALL OF SCHEEPJES MERION SOFT – COLOR 605 HOGARTH (COLOR C)

SCHEEPJES WHIRL FINE ART COMES IN CAKES OF 220G (7¾OZ) WITH A LENGTH OF 460M (503YDS) OF YARN. THE YARN CONSISTS OF 50% SUPERWASH MERINO WOOL/25% MICROFIBER/25% ACRYLIC YARN.

- 1 BALL OF SCHEEPJES WHIRL FINE ART – COLOR 661 ROCCOCO (COLOR B)

<u>SIZE OF PROJECT:</u> SINGLE REPEAT IN THE PATTERN WILL MEASURE APPROX. 7.5 X 7.5CM (3 X 3IN). THE FINISHED TABLE RUNNER WILL MEASURE ABOUT 125CM (49IN) IN LENGTH AND 35CM (14IN) IN WIDTH.

<u>SPECIAL STITCH IN THE PATTERN:</u> CRAB STITCH – WHICH IS AN SC MADE IN THE OPPOSITE DIRECTION YOU USUALLY WORK. IF YOU DON'T KNOW THIS STITCH, I SUGGEST LOOKING AT A VIDEO TUTORIAL TO UNDERSTAND IT BETTER.

<u>TIPS FOR THIS PATTERN:</u>

- TO CHANGE THIS PATTERN'S WIDTH, YOU CAN EASILY ADD OR REMOVE REPEATS TO THE DESIGN. FOR EACH REPETITION, YOU'LL ADD 16 STS TO THE PATTERN. FOR MORE OR LESS LENGTH, YOU CAN CROCHET MORE OR FEWER ROWS.

In Row 6 and 7, you'll start in the repeats with a ch1 and end with a ch1. However, when crocheting the repeats after each other in these Rows, they will form ch2-sps. So, at the beginning and the end of a Row, there is a ch1-sp; between the repeat sections, there will be a ch2-sp, which will come from the last ch1 of a repeat and the first ch1 of the next repeat.

R6 (RS): Pick up Color A in first st on Row at Right Side of work. Ch1, 1sc in next 2 sts, *ch1, sk next st, 1sc in next 4 sts, ch1, sk next st, 1dc, ch2, sk next 2 sts, 1dc, ch1, sk next st, 1sc in next 4 sts, ch1, sk next st. Rep from * 3 more times. 1sc in next 2 sts. Turn. [36sc/8dc/7 x ch2-sp/10 x ch1-sp]

R7 (WS): 1sc in next 2 sts, *ch1, sk next ch1-sp, 1sc in next 4 sts, ch1, sk next ch1-sp, 1sc in next st, ch2, sk next ch2-sp, 1sc in next st, ch1, sk next ch1-sp, 1sc in next 4 sts, ch1, sk next ch1-sp. Rep from * 3 more times. 1sc in next 2 sts. Put Color A aside. Turn work [44sc/7 x ch2-sp/10 x ch1-sp]

R8 (RS): Pick up Color B in first st on Row on the Right Side of the work. Ch1, 1sc in next 2 sts, *1dc, ch1, sk next st, 1sc in next 2 sts, ch1, sk next st, 1dc, ch1, sk next st, 2dc, ch1, sk next st, 1dc, ch1, sk next st, 1sc in next 2 sts, ch1, sk next st, 1dc. Rep from * 3 more times. 1sc in next 2 sts. Turn. [20sc/24dc/24 x ch1-sp]

- WHEN MAKING A DC IN THE PATTERN, YOU CROCHET THIS DC IN FRONT OF THE CH-SPS, IN THE SKIPPED ST UNDER IT. I JUST DESCRIBED A DC WITHOUT ANY FURTHER DIRECTIONS IN THE PATTERN, SO THE ABOVE INSTRUCTION APPLIES WHEN YOU CROCHET A DC. IF THERE ARE 2DC, YOU MAKE 1DC IN THE NEXT 2 SKIPPED STS.
- EACH COLOR CHANGE CONSISTS OF TWO ROWS – ONE ON THE RIGHT SIDE AND ONE ON THE WRONG SIDE. ON THE WRONG SIDE, WHEN YOU ENCOUNTER AN SC OR DC, YOU CROCHET SC IN IT; IF YOU ENCOUNTER A CH-SP, YOU CROCHET THE SAME AMOUNT OF CH-SP, SO YOU GET TWO CH-SPS RIGHT ABOVE EACH OTHER. THIS TECHNIQUE IS CALLED MOSAIC CROCHET. IT IS ONE OF THE TWO WAYS TO CROCHET MOSAIC.
- EACH TIME YOU CHANGE TO A DIFFERENT COLOR IN THE TWO-COLORED SECTIONS, YOU PUT ONE COLOR ASIDE, AND YOU PICK THE OTHER ONE UP IN THE FIRST ST. THIS COLOR-CHANGING ONLY HAPPENS ON ONE SIDE OF THE PATTERN AS YOU WILL CROCHET ONE RS ROW AND A WS ROW WITH THE SAME COLOR.
- THERE IS A CHART FOR THIS PATTERN, WHICH IS A SIMPLE ONE. IF YOU FIND IT TOO TRICKY, PLEASE STICK TO THE WRITTEN INSTRUCTIONS.
- AT THE END OF A RIGHT SIDE ROW, YOU WILL TURN YOUR WORK. YOU WILL DO THIS BY MAKING ONE CHAIN.

R9 (WS): 1sc in next 2 sts, *1sc in next st, ch1, sk next ch1-sp, 1sc in next 2 sts, ch1, sk next ch1-sp, 1sc in next st, ch1, sk next ch1-sp, 1sc in next 2 sts, ch1, sk next ch1-sp, 1sc in next st, ch1, sk next ch1-sp, 1sc in next 2 sts, ch1, sk next ch1-sp, 1sc in next st. Rep from * 3 more times. 1sc in next 2 sts. Put Color B aside. Turn work. [44sc/24 x ch1-sp]

In Row 10 and 11, you'll start in the repeats with a ch1 and end with a ch1. However, when crocheting the repeats after each other in these Rows, they will form ch2-sps. So, at the beginning and the end of a Row, there is a ch1-sp; between the repeat sections, there will be a ch2-sp, which comes from the last ch1 of a repeat and the first ch1 of the next repeat.

R10 (RS): Pick up Color A in first st on Row at Right Side of work. Ch1, 1sc in next 2 sts, *ch1, sk next st, 1dc, 1sc in next 2 sts, 1dc, 1sc in next st, 1dc, ch2, sk next 2 sts, 1dc, 1sc in next st, 1dc, 1sc in next 2 sts, 1dc, ch1, sk next st. Rep from * 3 more times. 1sc in next 2 sts. Turn. [28sc/24dc/7 x ch2-sp/2 x ch1-sp]

R11 (WS): 1sc in next 2 sts, *ch1, sk next ch1-sp, 1sc in next 6 sts, ch2, sk next ch2-sp, 1sc in next 6 sts, ch1, sk next ch1-sp. Rep from * 3 more times. 1sc in next 2 sts. Put Color A aside. Turn work. [52sc/7 x ch2-sp/2 x ch1-sp]

R12 (RS): Pick up Color B in first st on Row at Right Side of work. Ch1, 1sc in next 2 sts, *1dc, 1sc in next 3 sts, ch1, sk next st, 1sc in next 2 sts, 2dc, 1sc in next 2 sts, ch1, sk next st, 1sc in next 3 sts, 1dc. Rep from * 3 more times. 1sc in next 2 sts. Turn. [44sc/16dc/8 x ch1-sp]

R13 (WS): 1sc in next 2 sts, *1sc in next 4 sts, ch1, sk next ch1-sp, 1sc in next 6 sts, ch1, sk next st, 1sc in next 4 sts. Rep from * 3 more times. 1sc in next 2 sts. Put Color B aside. Turn work. [60sc/8 x ch1-sp]

R14 (RS): Pick up Color A in first st on Row at Right Side of work. Ch1, 1sc in next 2 sts, *1sc in next 4 sts, 1dc, ch1, sk next st, 1sc in next 4 sts, ch1, sk next st, 1dc, 1sc in next 4 sts. Rep from * 3 more times. 1sc in next 2 sts. Turn. [52sc/8dc/8 x ch1-sp]

R15 (WS): 1sc in next 2 sts, *1sc in next 5 sts, ch1, sk next ch1-sp, 1sc in next 4 sts, ch1, sk next ch1-sp, 1sc in next 5 sts. Rep from * 3 more times. 1sc in next 2 sts. Put Color A aside. Turn work. [60sc/8 x ch1-sp]

R16 (RS): Pick up Color B in first st on Row at Right Side of work. Ch1, 1sc in next 2 sts, *1sc in next 5 sts, 1dc, ch1, sk next st, 1sc in next 2 sts, ch1, sk next st, 1dc, 1sc in next 5 sts. Rep from * 3 more times. 1sc in next 2 sts. Turn. [52sc/8dc/8 x ch1-sp]

R17 (WS): 1sc in next 2 sts, *1sc in next 6 sts, ch1, sk next ch1-sp, 1sc in next 2 sts, ch1, sk next ch1-sp, 1sc in next 6 sts. Rep from * 3 more times. 1sc in next 2 sts. Put Color B aside. Turn work. [60sc/8 x ch1-sp]

R18 (RS): Pick up Color A in first st on Row at Right Side of work. Ch1, 1sc in next 2 sts, *1sc in next 5 sts, ch1, sk next st, 1dc, 1sc in next 2 sts, 1dc, ch1, sk next st, 1sc in next 5 sts. Rep from * 3 more times. 1sc in next 2 sts. Turn. [52sc/8dc/8 x ch1-sp]

R19 (WS): 1sc in next 2 sts, *1sc in next 5 sts, ch1, sk next ch1-sp, 1sc in next 4 sts, ch1, sk next ch1-sp, 1sc in next 5 sts. Rep from * 3 more times. 1sc in next 2 sts. Put Color A aside. Turn work. [60sc /8 x ch1-sp]

R20 (RS): Pick up Color B in first st on Row at Right Side of work. Ch1, 1sc in next 2 sts, *1sc in next 4 sts, ch1, sk next st, 1dc, 1sc in next 4 sts, 1dc, ch1, sk next st, 1sc in next 4 sts. Rep from * 3 more times. 1sc in next 2 sts. Turn. [52sc/8dc/8 x ch1-sp]

R21 (WS): 1sc in next 2 sts, *1sc in next 4 sts, ch1, sk next ch1-sp, 1sc in next 6 sts, ch1, sk next ch1-sp, 1sc in next 4 sts. Rep from * 3 more times. 1sc in next 2 sts. Put Color B aside. Turn work. [60sc/8 x ch1-sp]

In Row 22 and 23, you'll start in the repeats with a ch1 and end with a ch1. However, when crocheting the repeats after each other in these Rows, they will form ch2-sps. So, at the beginning and the end of a Row, there is a ch1-sp; between the repeat sections, there will be a ch2-sp, which come from the last ch1 of a repeat and the first ch1 of the next repeat.

R22 (RS): Pick up Color A in first st on Row at Right Side of work. Ch1, 1sc in next 2 sts, *ch1, sk next st, 1sc in next 3 sts, 1dc, 1sc in next 2 sts, ch2, sk next 2 sts, 1sc in next 2 sts, 1dc, 1sc in next 3 sts, ch1, sk next st. Rep from * 3 more times. 1sc in next 2 sts. Turn. [44sc/8dc/7 x ch2-sp/2 x ch1-sp]

R23 (WS): 1sc in next 2 sts, *ch1, sk next ch1-sp, 1sc in next 6 sts, ch2, sk next ch2-sp, 1sc in next 6 sts, ch1, sk next ch1-sp. Rep from * 3 more times. 1sc in next 2 sts. Put Color A aside. Turn work. [52sc/7 x ch2-sp/2 x ch1-sp]

R24 (RS): Pick up Color B in first st on Row at Right Side of work. Ch1, 1sc in next 2 sts, *1dc, ch1, sk next st, 1sc in next 2 sts, ch1, sk next st, 1sc in next st, ch1, sk next st, 2dc, ch1, sk next st, 1sc in next st, ch1, sk next st, 1sc in next 2 sts, ch1, sk next st, 1dc. Rep from * 3 more times. 1sc in next 2 sts. Turn. [28sc/16dc/24 x ch1-sp]

R25 (WS): 1sc in next 2 sts, *1sc in next st, ch1, sk next ch1-sp, 1sc in next 2 sts, ch1, sk next ch1-sp, 1sc in next st, ch1, sk next ch1-sp, 1sc in next 2 sts, ch1, sk next ch1-sp, 1sc in next st, ch1, sk next ch1-sp, 1sc in next 2 sts, ch1, sk next ch1-sp, 1sc in next st. Rep from * 3 more times. 1sc in next 2 sts. Put Color B aside. Turn work. [44sc/24 x ch1-sp]

In Row 26 and 27, you'll start in the repeats with a ch1 and end with a ch1. However, when crocheting the repeats after each other in these Rows, they will form ch2-sps. So, at the beginning and the end of a Row, there is a ch1-sp; between the repeat sections, there will be a ch2-sp, which comes from the last ch1 of a repeat and the first ch1 of the next repeat.

R26 (RS): Pick up Color A in first on Row at Right Side of work. Ch1, 1sc in next 2 sts, *ch1, sk next st, 1dc, 1sc in next 2 sts, 1dc, ch1, sk next st, 1dc, ch2, sk next 2 sts, 1dc, ch1, sk next st, 1dc, 1sc in next 2 sts, 1dc, ch1, sk next st. Rep from * 3 more times. 1sc in next 2 sts. Turn. [20sc/24dc/7 x ch2-sp/10 x ch1-sp]

R27 (WS): 1sc in next 2 sts, *ch1, sk next ch1-sp, 1sc in next 4 sts, ch1, sk next ch1-sp, 1sc in next st, ch2, sk next ch2-sp, 1sc in next st, ch1, sk next ch1-sp, 1sc in next 4 sts, ch1, sk next ch1-sp. Rep from * 3 more times. 1sc in next 2 sts. Put Color A aside. Turn work. [44sc/7 x ch2-sp/10 x ch1-sp]

R28 (RS): Pick up Color B in first st on Row at Right Side of work. Ch1, 1sc in next 2 sts, *1dc, 1sc in next 4 sts, 1dc, ch1, sk next st, 2dc, ch1, sk next st, 1dc, 1sc in next 4 sts, 1dc. Rep from * 3 more times. 1sc in next 2 sts. Turn. [36sc/24dc/8 x ch1-sp]

R29 (WS): 1sc in next 2 sts, *1sc in next 6 sts, ch1, sk next ch1-sp, 1sc in next 2 sts, ch1, sk next st, 1sc in next 6 sts. Rep from * 3 more times. 1sc in next 2 sts. Put Color B aside. Turn work. [60sc/8 x ch1-sp]

To continue, you keep repeating **Rows 6-29** until most of the yarn is used up. When you have about 10g (⅓oz) left of both colors, it is time to end the pattern. It doesn't matter which Row you finish the pattern with, as long as you end with a Color A Row and the following directions:

- Crochet the first Color A Row – make the sc stitches and the dc stitches as normal and change the ch stitches to for regular sc stitches.
- Crochet the second Color A Row, which will be a Row of just sc stitches.
- Crochet another two Rows of sc stitches, turning the work each Row. Once you finished these four Rows with Color A, fasten off Color A.

The Border:
The only thing left to do is crochet a border around the table runner. I didn't write down the total amount of stitches in this section so that the edge applies to any size made out of this pattern. You crochet at the top and bottom of the table runner in the regular stitches, which are already there; you crochet sc stitches in the rows at the long sides. I crocheted one sc for every two Rows of the pattern. Also, use the larger hook for the border: the 4.5mm (7) hook size and Color C.

In the first Round, you attach the yarn in a corner where you make a ch to start and then crochet 3sc. As it depends on a right or left-handed crocheter, the side you start on can be different. If you work a short side, work sc stitches in the sts already there; if you work a long side, make an sc for every two Rows. In every corner, you make 3sc. When you have worked your way around, you make an ss in the first st to connect and ss to the second st in the 3sc-gr.

In the second Round, you do the same as the first border Round; only you now work the 3sc in each middle sc of a 3sc-gr of the first Round. Between those corners, you work sc stitches in the sc stitches of the first Round. When you have worked your way around it, make an ss in first st to connect.

In the third Round, you'll make a crab stitch in each st of Round. And yes, this means you work in the opposite direction to which you usually crochet. After you completed this, fasten off yarn and weave in all ends.

Ensure you block the table runner in straight lines to keep the pattern in line for a perfect outcome.

29	x					x	O	x	x	O	x					x	28
27	O	x			x	O	x	O	O	x	O	x			x	O	26
25	x	O			O		O	x	x	O		O			O	x	24
23	O				x			O	O			x				O	22
21					O	x					x	O					20
19						O	x			x	O						18
17						x	O			O	x						16
15					x	O					O	x					14
13	x				O			x	x			O				x	12
11	O	x			x		x	O	O	x		x			x	O	10
9	x	O			O	x	O	x	x	O	x	O			O	x	8
7	O					O	x	O	O	x	O					O	6
5							O			O							4
	16	15	14	13	12	11	10	9	8	7	6	5	4	3	2	1	

The chart is pretty straightforward. All the even Rows are where you work sc, dc, or chains. A blank box indicates an sc, an 'x' indicates a dc, and an O indicates chains.

All the odd Rows are the similar but crocheted on the Wrong Side of the work. Make an sc in each sc or dc from the previous row and make ch-sps over the ch-sps of the previous row using the same amount of chs.

IN MALBORK, YOU
WILL FIND THE
TEUTONIC ORDER'S
CASTLE

SOME WORDS OF GRATITUDE...

For a long time, I wondered if what I created was good enough to share with the world. To be placed among other great names in this industry was something I was unsure about. Although many crafters from all over the world gave me credit every day and told me my work was different from the standard, that my color choices are exquisite, and they only wanted more, I still doubted myself. I could never have imagined the day would come when I would find the courage to write a book. That day finally arrived but it would be a lie to say I did this all by myself. So it is time to say thanks to some influential people who supported me in this personal journey.

Firstly, a huge thanks to Loes from Livres de Louise, my publisher, and Alexa Boonstra, the author and creator behind crochet and knitting blog, Amilishly. I sent Loes a crazy idea to combine travel stories with crochet patterns in a book. She immediately believed in the concept and that I was the one who could bring it to life. Without her, this book would never have existed. And the reason for even writing a book came from Alexa. She paved my first steps for me by telling me what it meant to write a crochet book. I'm sure you will agree that these two wonderful ladies definitely deserve a lot of gratitude.

Secondly, I want to thank the yarn manufacturer Scheepjes, who kindly sponsored the yarn for this book. They made it possible to create each pattern in the best way by providing me with the right tools. I want to thank the creative director of Scheepjes, Simy Somer, in particular. She told me that what I was doing with yarn deserved a bigger audience and that I needed to believe more in what I did. She still supports me and I know I can always count on a professional and clear answer from her whenever I have a crochet-related issue.

Lastly, I want to thank my mother, Anja, for her full support every hour of the day. She took various household chores off my plate while I was writing this book and she even acted as my pattern tester. Speaking of testing, I want to thank Tineke from the bottom of my heart. For some years now, she has been my guiding light when it comes to testing and translation jobs. Every pattern in this book is checked and crocheted by her as well. Thank you, Tineke. As well as Tineke, a whole test team gave their full attention to make sure the book's patterns are correct. Each of them deserves a huge thank you for the work they have accomplished.

I do hope you have enjoyed reading this book and making something from it. I hope you feel like you've discovered more about our beautiful world without the need to leave your home. If this is how you feel, then my job is done.

Mark

Special thanks to my testers: Anja, Tineke, Anna Nilson, Christina Berberich, Wendy de Vries, Geertje van de Valk, Marieke van Dijk, Else Linde, Eveline Heemskerk-Verhoeven, Caroline Tigchelaar, Carina de Paepe-Verblauw, Hetty van der Meulen-Blankhorst, Annemieke Keuning, Susan Badoux van Dieren, Anita Mooi-Feenstra, Jade Moors, Izilda Garcez Capovilla, Christa Rusbach, Marjan Tilly, Bertje Broekmeulen, Lisette van Oversteeg, Iris Wiegertjes, Marinka Grünbauer, Ingeborg Hendriks, Kippie van de Merwe-Graafland, Marion Bogers-Pettinga

A DAVID AND CHARLES BOOK

David and Charles is an imprint of David and Charles, Ltd, Suite A, Tourism House, Pynes Hill, Exeter, EX2 5WS

First published in the Netherlands and the UK by Livres de Louise in 2021 as Journey: A Book from The Guy with the Hook. This edition first published in the UK and USA by David and Charles, Ltd in 2022.

A catalogue record for this book is available from the British Library.

ISBN-13: 9781446309568 paperback
ISBN-13: 9781446382226 EPUB
ISBN-13: 9781446382219 PDF

This book has been printed on paper from approved suppliers and made from pulp from sustainable sources.

Printed in UK by Short Run Press for:
David and Charles, Ltd
Suite A, Tourism House, Pynes Hill, Exeter, EX2 5WS

10 9 8 7 6 5 4 3 2 1

Livres de Louise
www.livresdelouise.nl

The Guy with the Hook
www.theguywiththehook.com

Patterns and text: Mark Roseboom
Photography: Peggy Janssen
Styling: Claire Eversdijk
Design: StudioBont
Illustrations: Burunduk's, Luckyrizki, Simple Line, Singleline, Valenty/Shutterstock.com
Yarn sponsor: Scheepjes

David and Charles publishes high-quality books on a wide range of subjects. For more information visit www.davidandcharles.com.

Share your makes with us on social media using #dandcbooks and follow us on Facebook and Instagram by searching for @dandcbooks.

Layout of the digital edition of this book may vary depending on reader hardware and display settings.